Chinese Seafood

Author: Huang Su-Huei
Translator: Lai Yen-Jen
Editor: Gloria C. Martinez
Publisher: Huang Su-Huei
Dishes prepared by: Lee Mu-Tsun
Hsu Wen-Shun, Hai Pa Wang Restaurant (Taiwan)
Hung Po-Wei, Hai Tsun Restaurant (Taiwan)
Wu Ming, Jum Bo Restaurant (Taiwan)
Lin Mao-Sheng
Designers Shaw, Haizan
Wang Chin-Kuang
Photographers: Aki Ohno
Wu Hua-Sheng
Typesetting: Graphics Express
Printed by: China Color Printing Co., Inc.

ISBN: 0-941676-09-9

introduction to **Lee Mu-Tsun**

Mr. Lee was born in Taipei, Taiwan. He expressed an interest in food preparation at an early age. He attended classes at Wei-Chuan's Department of Home Economics and later became an instructor of cooking classes at Wei-Chuan. As an instructor, he taught cooking classes for three years on television in Taiwan.

Mr. Lee was also a professor of Chinese cooking at the Tsuji Academy Japan Cooking School for three years. In 1969, Mr. Lee joined Wei-Chuan and has assisted in publishing "Chinese Cuisine", "Chinese Snacks", "Chinese Cooking for Beginners", and "Chinese Appetizers and Garnishes".

Introduction

It is twenty-three years since I took charge of Wei-Chuan's Cooking. I wish to acknowledge with thanks all the wonderful people who have helped Wei-Chuan grow and maintain its high standards. I can not list the names of all the persons who have been supportive of my efforts because they are numerous, however, I must mention Mr. Lee Mu-Tsun, who has provided so much assistance with his expertise in cookery. Mr. Lee has been with me for 15 years. He has not only assisted with Wei-Chuan's Cookbooks and served as instructor of cooking classes, but he has also assisted Wei-Chuan, USA to develop new food products. Mr. Lee's great interest in fishing and seafood cooking have been invaluable to me in writing this book.

"Chinese Seafood" is published in two editions, Chinese and English. Recipes include ingredients that are readily available. Various cooking methods are used and substitute ingredients are suggested to adapt the recipes to different geographical areas. This book will lend itself to creating your own variations of dishes. After the basic techniques are learned, new, colorful, aromatic, and tasty seafood dishes may be developed.

Comments and recommendations regarding this book are most welcome.

Huang Su Huei

August, 1984

1

TABLE OF CONTENTS

● Fish

● Others

● Soup

Table of Measurements

1 Cup (1 C.)
236 c.c.

1 Tablespoon (1 T.)
15 c.c.

1 Teaspoon (1 t.)
5 c.c.

Seasoning Used to Prepare Chinese Food

Five kinds of seasonings are frequently used to prepare Chinese food: salt, MSG, pepper, sugar, and sesame oil. Wine, vinegar, cornstarch, and oil for frying, etc., are also necessary.

Soy sauce

Sesame oil
Vinegar

Oil for frying
(Fried Oil)

Cornstarch

Rice wine

Sugar

Salt   Black pepper

Utensils Used to Prepare Chinese Dishes

Cleavers, chopping block, spatulas, wok, and steamers are basic utensils used to prepare Chinese food. A rolling pin, for rolling dumplings, a sifter, and a hand-mixer are also used to prepare Chinese snacks. An iron skillet or frying pan may also be used to cook Chinese food. Roasting, frying, steaming, and stewing are techniques used to prepare a wide variety of delicious food.

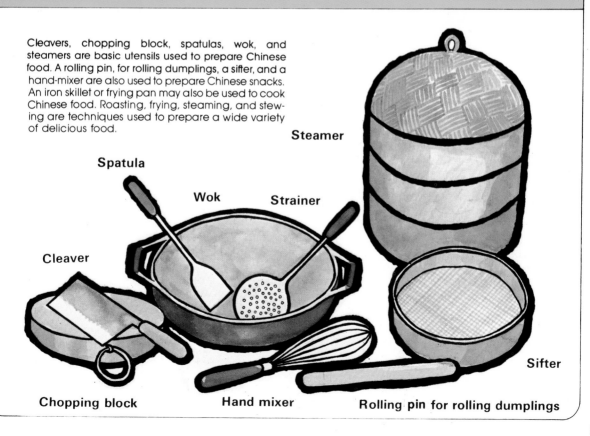

Steamer

Spatula

Wok   Strainer

Cleaver

Sifter

Chopping block   Hand mixer   Rolling pin for rolling dumplings

5

Culinary Idioms

Chinese cooking is a very subjective art. There are no definite quantities of any ingredients, nor any exact time limits for cooking any recipe. We encourage you to develop this art through trial and error. We have listed the basic information for the preparation of all dishes, as well as the ingredients needed; however, we encourage you to adapt the recipes to your own taste. In order that you may further understand the practice of Chinese cuisine, we give significant points and explain some expressions used often in Chinese cooking.

CLEANING

Clean the ingredients before using them, then drain and dry them thoroughly.

CUTTING

All ingredients must be cut into the same size and shape, so that the cooked food will look uniform and have the same tenderness.

PRE-SEASONING

Chicken, pork, beef, fish, and shrimp must be marinated in the prescribed sauces to enhance the taste of the food. Coat with egg white and cornstarch to increase tenderness.

MIXING

If no cooking is required, just mix the ingredients together after cutting. If ingredients have been precooked, allow them to cool, then mix them together; add sauce and serve.

STIR-FRYING

To put the material into a very hot wok over high heat and turn over and over, until done.

Stir-frying is a very quick process. It is advisable to prepare all of the sauces in advance, including the cornstarch and water used to thicken the final sauce.

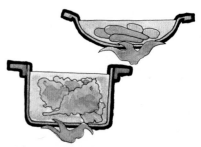

When several kinds of ingredients are used in cooking, the difference in tenderness of each ingredient will sometimes require that material be cooked in oil, boiled, or fried before mixing. Whichever method is used, the ingredient must be precooked till tender.

When the preliminary preparation is finished, heat the wok and pour in oil. Add the onion, ginger root or garlic and stir until they impart their aroma. Add the ingredients, and a few drops of wine, if desired, to enhance the flavor of the food. Add the sauce and stir-fry until all ingredients are mixed together. This entire process must be short and quick so that the food will not overcook.

At this point, you may sprinkle a few drops of oil on the food. This will help to increase the brilliancy of the food and help to keep it warm

DEEP-FRYING

To immerse the food in deep, hot oil.

Prepare the material for frying; first the food must be marinated in the prescribed sauce, then coated with the proper flour or cornstarch batter.

There should be plenty of oil in the pan, enough to cover the material. However, if the material to be fried is very juicy or contains a lot of moisture, the oil should not occupy more than 60% of the work so that it will not splash out of the wok.

First boil the oil; remove the wok from the heat and when the oil has cooled to medium temperature, put the food into the wok. Replace the wok over medium heat and cook until near-tender. Then turn heat to high and cook over high heat until done. This seals the flavor and ensures that the food will be completely cooked and crispy on the outside.

All food put into the oil at the same time must be removed at the same time to maintain uniformity.

STEAMING

To put the material in a steaming cage which is then put on a wok containing boiling water.

First, put water in the wok and allow it to come to a boil.

Then place food in the cage and put it on the wok

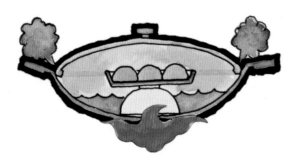

Simple method for steaming: Place a bowl, upside down, on the bottom of the wok; add water (water should not cover the bowl). Put a heatproof plate on the bowl and place food on the heatproof plate, cover and steam.

MIX-BOIL

First, put the sauce or soup into the wok by itself and allow it to boil, then add the food. The amount of cornstarch in the sauce should be to your own taste; however, there should not be too much sauce.

STEWING

Stewing is similar to steaming. Put water in a large pot. Put material and water or stock, to cover, in a smaller pot and set it inside the large pot. Cook over a moderate heat until the food is tender. Soup prepared this way is very clear.

SMOKING

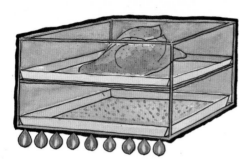

Put food in an oven (or cover and place on a grill); throw sugar, wood powder, or tea leaves into the fire or oven so that the fumes will smoke the food and give it flavor.

ROASTING

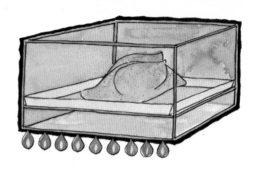

Cook or bake food in the oven with all the ingredients, until done.

PRECOOKING

Place ingredients in hot oil or hot water for several seconds, or until slightly tender, then remove. (Pork, beef, chicken, fish, or shrimp is usually sliced or shredded, seasoned, and coated with cornstarch before precooking.)

oil out

Preparing the wok:
Heat the wok then place 4 Tbsp. oil in wok and swirl it in wok to cover lower two-thirds of surface; remove excess oil. (This will prevent ingredients from sticking.)

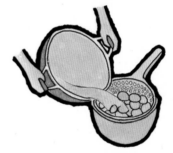

Reheat wok and add enough oil to cover ingredients; heat oil until hot but not smoking. Add food. Stir quickly to Separate ingredients; stir-fry until ingredients change color then remove. (Add 1 Tbsp. oil to ingredients and stir before frying. The ingredients will separate easily.)

STOCK

Broth from boiled Pork, beef, or chicken meat or bones.

Boil water in a large pot; add pork, beef, or chicken meat or bones to boiling water. Remove. Discard water. (Purpose: to clean the meat.)

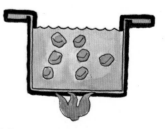

Put clean water in the pot and add the pork, beef, or chicken meat or bones. Bring to a boil and remove any scum. After removing scum, lower heat to medium. Add two green onions, two slices of ginger root, and one tablespoon wine. Cook for one hour. Remove pork, beef, or chicken. Stock is ready for use.

Preparing Fish

1. Scale fish.
2. Cut along the belly of the fish.
3. Make a cut between the head and the gill; do not cut through.
4. Remove and discard the gills and the entrails.
5. Cut off the head before filleting.
6. Cut from the back or the belly of the fish.
7. Cut by sliding the blade along backbone and over ribs.
8. Release the flesh in one piece.
9. Use the same procedure to release the other side.
10. Cut off and discard the flesh that surrounded the belly. It is the least desirable part of the fish and has an offensive smell.
11. Skin the fillet.

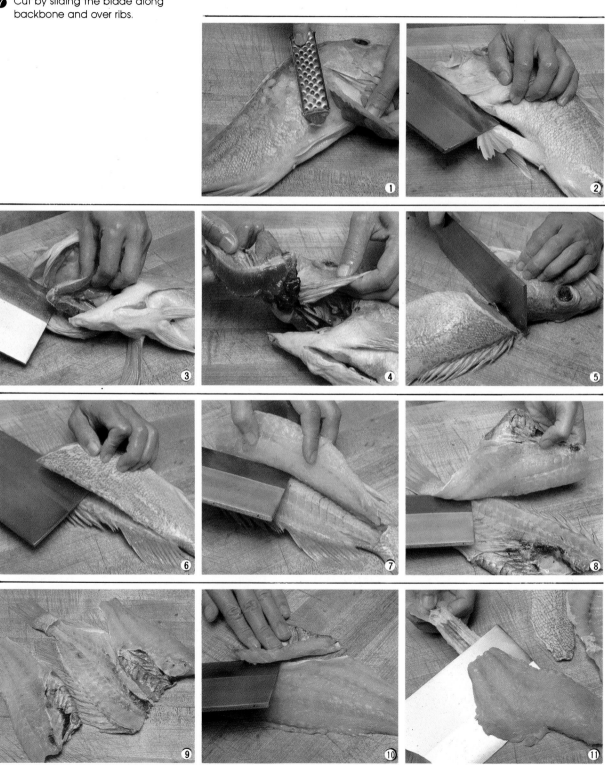

Preparing Clams

❶ Mix 1 t. salt and 1 c. water.
❷ Pour the salt solution over the clams. The water does not have to cover the clams completely. Soak the clams for several hours until they release the sand.

Preparing Crab

❶ Pour boiling water over the live crab.
❷ Cut the crab in half at the center.
❸ Open the shell and remove the gills of the crab.

❹ Cut off the legs and claws of the crab.
❺ Cut the body of the crab into pieces.
❻ Crack the shells of the claws and legs with a mallet.

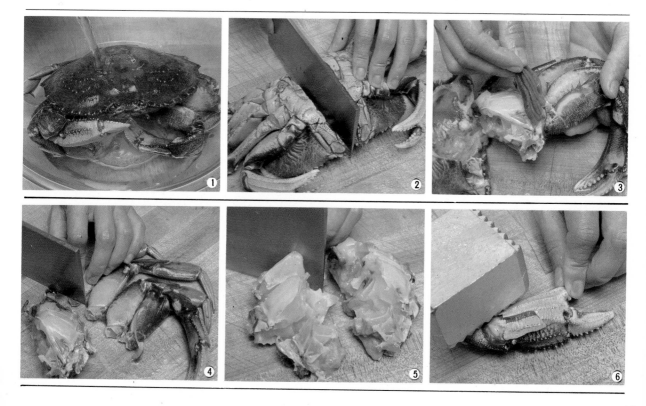

Preparing Shrimp

❶ Use a toothpick to devein the shrimp.
❷ Remove the shell from the shrimp. Add ½ t. salt and 1 T. water to ½ lb. shrimp; mix lightly. Rinse the shrimp then drain.
❸ Slice the large shrimp in half.
❹ To marinate, add ¼ t. salt and 1 T. wine to ½ lb. shrimp.
❺ Mix until marinade is completely absorbed.
❻ To increase the stickness of the shrimp add ½ egg white and mix well.
❼ Add cornstarch and mix. Cornstarch is added to keep the moisture in the shrimp.
❽ Add 1 T. oil to the shrimp and mix well before frying so that the shrimp will separate easily during frying.

Preparing Squid

❶ Pull out the long, transparent, sword-shaped shell.
❷ Separate the body from the hood.
❸ Pull out the head and discard all material that easily comes free from the body.
❹ Cut the head in half then gently remove the eyes and the beak of the squid. Wash the squid.
❺ Cut the squid to open the body.
❻ Peel off the membrane from the hood.
❼ Cut the squid lengthwise into strips.
❽ Make diagonal cuts to ⅔ deep on the inside surface.
❾ Turn the squid and make diagonal cuts to ⅔ deep to form diamond-shape cuts.
   Cut the squid into pieces.
❿ Plunge the squid into boiling water; it will curl.

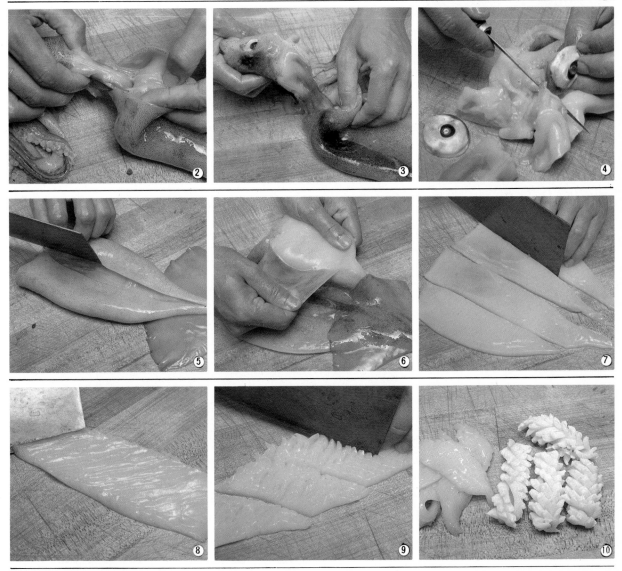

烤 卵 魚
Baked Shisamo

烤 赤 鯮
Baked Snapper

14

Baked Shisamo

12 shisamo
½ T. cooking wine
pinch of salt
6 wooden or steel skewers
½ lemon

❶ Choose large shishamo that have large abdomens (the more eggs the better). Clean the shisamo; there is no need to remove foreign matter. Thread a skewer through the head, body then tail of two shisamo. Prepare the remaining shishamo in the same manner. Sprinkle them with wine and salt.

❷ Preheat oven to 450°F. Place a piece of aluminum foil on a pan; grease the foil with oil. Put the shishamo on the pan. Bake at 450° for 12 minutes or until the fish is golden brown and the eggs expand. Sprinkle with lemon juice, if desired.

■ Shishamo comes from Japan. Frozen shishamo can be bought in the United States, especially in Japanese markets. Salted and unsalted frozen shishamo are sold in the United States. Do not add salt before baking, if the salted one is used.

> Snapper, halfbeak (Fig. 1), beltfish (Fig. 2), and other kinds of fish may be used for baking.

Baked Snapper

1 whole snapper (about 1⅓ lbs.)
① { 1 T. cooking wine
    1 t. salt
1 wooden or steel skewer
½ lemon

❶ Clean the fish. Make a few diagonal cuts through the meat along the spine. Marinate the fish in ① for 20 minutes; drain. Thread a skewer through the head, body then tail of the fish. Spread some salt over the fins of the fish to prevent burning during baking.

❷ Preheat oven to 500°F. Put the fish in a pan and bake it on the middle rack of the oven for 20 minutes. Sprinkle lemon juice over the fish, if desired.

■ The fish is cooked when the eyes turn white.

烤 鰻 魚
Baked Eel

烤 魷 魚
Baked Squid

16

Smoked and Baked Fish Fillets

1　lb. fish fillets

① { 1　T. each: cooking wine, sugar
4　T. soy sauce
2　t. salt
4　green onions, pressed
4　slices ginger root, mashed

② { ½　c. tea
2　T. sugar

❶ Cut fish into large pieces and marinate it with ① for at least 20 minutes.
❷ Grease the top rack of the oven.
❸ Preheat oven to 500°F. Put the fish on the greased rack. Put ② on a pan then put the pan on the bottom rack. Bake the fish for 30 minutes; remove and sprinkle with sesame oil.
■ Ingredients ② may be omitted to eliminate "smoking" of fish. Flounder (sole), kingfish, or other kinds of fish may be used for this recipe.

Smoked and Baked Whole Fish

1　whole fish (about 1⅔ lbs.)
Ingredients ① and ② are the same as ① and ② of "Smoked and Baked Fish Fillet"

❶ Clean the fish. Place it on a cutting surface. Hold the knife horizontally and cut lengthwise from the outside toward the bone to butterfly. Marinate the fish in ① for 6 hours.
❷ Other steps are the same as steps ❷ and ❸ of "Smoked and Baked Fish Fillet".

Baked Eel

1　eel

① { 4　T. soy sauce
2　T. cooking wine
3　T. sugar
½　c. water

3　wooden or steel skewers (4-6 inches long)

❶ Remove the backbone of the eel. Cut the eel crosswise in half. Thread the skewers lengthwise from the head to the middle and from the middle of the bottom half to the tail. Thread the skewer through both halves at the center and at both sides of the eel. This will prevent their curling during baking. Cook ① for 6 minutes or until liquid thickens.
❷ Preheat oven to 550°F. Bake the fish on the middle rack of the oven for 20 minutes or until both sides are dried (Turn the fish over during baking.) Spread half of ① on one side of the fish and bake for 5 minutes. Turn the fish over; spread the remaining portion of ① on the other side of the fish and bake for another 5 minutes.

Baked Squid

1　large squid (about 1⅓ lbs.)
1　T. cooking wine

① { 1　t. sesame seeds
¾　t. salt
dash of pepper

½　lemon

❶ Cut the squid lengthwise to butterfly. Remove the eyes and the foreign matter of the squid. Clean, drain, and score the inside surface of the squid. Marinate the squid with wine for 10 minutes. Remove and pat dry before baking. Put the squid, skin side down, on a rack; sprinkle with .①
❷ Preheat oven to 550°F. Bake the squid on the middle rack of the oven for 10 minutes or until golden brown. Sprinkle with lemon juice, if desired.

烤 醬 魚
Baked Fish Fillets with Bean Paste

酥 小 魚
Crispy Fis

Baked Fish Fillets with Bean Paste

1 lb. fish fillets
① { ½ c. miso or bean paste
4 T. sugar
2 T. cooking wine
½ lemon
sesame oil

❶ Rinse the fish and pat it dry; cut it into pieces. Marinate the fish with ① for 1 day.

❷ Preheat oven to 500°F. Line a baking pan with a piece of aluminum foil. Remove any marinade from the fish; place the fish on the baking pan. Reserve the marinade if desired. Bake the fish on the middle rack of the oven for 12 minutes or until golden brown. Spread some sesame oil over the fish. Sprinkle with lemon juice and serve.

■ Kingfish or other kinds of fish may be used for this recipe. The ingredients in ① may be saved for future use. To reuse, bring it to a boil then let it cool.

Fish with Vinegar Sauce

15 small fish (about 2⅔ lbs.)   oil
① { 3 T. cooking wine
1¼ t. salt
6 T. cornstarch
② { 1½ c. water
¾ c. each: sugar, vinegar, cooking wine
⅓ c. each: soy sauce, lemon juice
1 T. each: salt, Szechuan peppercorns (or ½ t. pepper)
3 hot peppers
3 green onions
3 slices ginger root

❶ Clean the fish then make a few deep cuts on the thick part of the body. Marinate the fish in ① for at least 10 minutes. Remove and pat dry; coat the fish with cornstarch.

❷ Bring ② to a boil then turn off the heat.

❸ Heat the wok then add oil. Deep-fry the fish for 6 minutes until they float and are golden brown; remove. Marinate the fish in ② while they are still hot. Refrigerate when they are cool; marinate for at least 24 hours. Turn the fish over during marinating. The fish may be refriferated for 4 or 5 days and serve as desired.

> To prevent the fish from sticking together, deep-fry in batches of 5 or 8 fish at a time. Remove the fish when they are dry. Follow the same steps until all the fish are fried. reheat the wok. Put all the fish into the wok then deep-fry for 6 minutes or until crispy. Smelt, small kingfish or other kinds of small fish are suitable for "Fish with Vinegar Sauce" and "Crispy Fish"

Crispy Fish

15 small fish (about 2⅔ lbs.)
① { 1 T. soy sauce
3 T. cooking wine
1 t. salt
oil
② { 1½ T. each: chopped green onions, chopped ginger root
1 T. each: chopped garlic, crushed hot pepper (or hot bean paste)
③ { 2 T. each: cooking wine, soy sauce, vinegar
1 T. each: sugar, sesame oil
2 T. water

❶ Clean the fish and make a few deep cuts on the thick part of the fish. Marinate the fish with ① for 20 minutes; remove and pat dry.

❷ Heat the wok then add oil. Deep-fry the fish for 6 minutes or until they are crispy; remove. Remove the oil.

❸ Reheat the wok then add 1 T. oil. Stir-fry ② until fragrant. Add ③ and the fish; stir-fry until the liquid has almost evaporated. This dish may be served hot or cold.

Deep-fried Fish

2⅔ lbs. fish
① the same as ingredients ① of "Crispy Fish" (½ t. five-spice powder may be added)
oil
② { 2 green onions
2 slices ginger root
4 T. each: soy sauce, cooking wine, sugar
2 hot red peppers or dried hot peppers
3 c. water
2 t. vinegar
2 T. sesame oil

❶ Clean the fish and pat them dry. Cut the fish into 1 inch thick steaks; marinate in ① for at least 1 hour. Remove and pat dry before deep-frying.

❷ Heat the wok then add oil. Deep-fry the fish for 6 minutes or until crispy; remove. Remove the oil.

❸ Put the fish and ② in the wok; bring to a boil. Continue to cook for 15 minutes or until the liquid has almost evaporated. Sprinkle with sesame oil. Turn the fish over; cook until the liquid has evaporated.

■ Do not stir the fish during cooking because it flakes easily. This dish may be refrigerated for 4 or 5 days and served hot or cold.

炸鱔魚
Deep-fried Smelt

酥炸溪魚
Crispy Smelt

Deep-fried Smelt

1 lb. smelt
① { ½ T. cooking wine
    ½ t. salt
    dash of pepper
1 egg yolk
1½ T. cornstarch
oil
dipping sauce: Szechuan peppercorn salt or
               ketchup

❶ Clean the smelt and marinate them with ① for 10 minutes; remove and pat dry. Mix the smelt with egg yolk and cornstarch.

❷ Heat the wok then add oil. Deep-fry the smelt for 4 minutes or until golden brown; remove. Serve the smelt with dipping sauce.

■ The fishmeat will be crispier and the fish will become smaller by following this recipe. This dish may be served hot or cold.

Deep-fried Beltfish

❶ Ingredients and steps are the same as for "Deep-fried Smelt", except substitute beltfish for smelt.

❷ **The handling of beltfish:** Clean the fish; use a brush to remove the clear coating from the skin of the fish. Rinse the fish then pat it dry; cut it into pieces. Make a few cuts on the surface of the fish then marinate it in ① for 10 minutes. Remove and pat dry the fish; mix it with egg yolk and cornstarch. Deep-fry the fish. If the fish is served with rice, increase the salt in ingredients ①

Crispy Smelt

1 lb. smelt
① { ½ T. cooking wine
    ½ t. salt
    dash of pepper
oil
② { ¾ c. water
    ½ T. sugar
    ½ t. baking powder
    1 c. flour
    1 T. each: sesame seeds, oil
dipping sauce: ketchup or Szechuan peppercorn salt
1 lemon

❶ Clean the smelt and marinate them with ① for 10 minutes. Mix ② to a batter.

❷ Heat the wok then add oil. Pat dry the smelt and coat them with the flour batter. Deep-fry the smelt for 4 minutes or until golden brown; remove. Serve the smelt with dipping sauce. Sprinkle lemon juice over the smelt. if desired.

■ It is best to serve this dish hot to retain a crispy skin. If cool, the moisture of the fish will soften the coating and make it soggy.

Crispy Small Fish

● Any kind of small fish is suitable for this dish. Other ingredients and steps are the same as for "Crispy Smelt".

糖 醋 帶 魚
Sweet and Sour Beltfish

台 式 醋 魚
Taiwanese-style Fish with Vinegar Sauce

Sweet and Sour Beltfish

1⅓ lbs. beltfish, middle section

① {
1 T. cooking wine
1 t. salt
}

1 egg yolk
6 T. cornstarch

oil

② {
5 T. sugar
6 T. water
4 T. vinegar
2 T. ketchup
1 T. each: cooking wine, sesame oil
½ T. cornstarch
¾ t. salt
}

糖醋醬

③ {
2 T. shredded green onions
2 T. coriander
1 whole hot pepper, shredded
}

❶ Remove the foreign matter from athe fish. Use a brush to remove the clear coating from the skin of the fish. Make diagonal cuts through the meat to the bone at every 1½ inches on both sides of the fish. Marinate the fish in ① for at least 20 minutes.

❷ Remove and pat dry the fish. Coat the fish, including inside of cuts, with egg yolk then with cornstarch. Heat the wok then add oil. Deep-fry the fish for 7 minutes or until golden brown; remove and put it on a plate.

❸ Bring ② to a boil; pour it over the fish. Sprinkle the fish with ③

■ Other kinds of fish are suitable for this dish (see Fig. 1).

Pinecone-shaped Fish

● See "Sweet and Sour Beltfish" for ingredients. Cut the fish to butterfly it; remove the fish bones. Score the inside surface of the fish lengthwise and crosswise. Coat the fish with egg yolk then cornstarch. Deep-fry it until golden brown; remove and put it on a plate. Bring ② to a boil; sprinkle it over the fish (see Fig. 2). (Onions, carrots or green peas may be added to ingredients ②)

Taiwanese-style Fish with Vinegar Sauce

1 fish (about 1⅓ lbs.)

① {
1 T. cooking wine
½ t. salt
}

oil

② {
3 T. soy sauce
1 T. vinegar
½ T. each: sesame oil, sugar
½ T. each: chopped ginger root, chopped garlic
2 T. chopped green onions
1 hot pepper, sliced
}

❶ Clean the fish then make shallow cuts on the surface. Marinate the fish with ① for 20 minutes; pat dry before deep-frying.

❷ Heat the wok then add oil. Deep-fry the fish for 6 minutes or until golden brown; remove and put it on a plate.

❸ Pour ② over the fish while the fish is still hot.

Fried Fish

1 fish (about 1⅓ lbs.)

① {
1 T. cooking wine
½ t. salt
2 T. flour
}

② dipping sauce: {
3 T. vinegar or lemon juice
1½ T. chopped ginger root
⅓ t. salt
}

❶ See step ❶ of "Taiwanese-style Fish with Vinegar Sauce". Coat the fish with cornstarch after marinating.

❷ Heat the wok then add 3 T. oil. Rotate the wok to distrubute the oil around the wok. Fry the fish until both sides are golden brown; remove and serve with dipping sauce.

豆瓣鯰魚
Catfish with
Bean Paste Sauce

乾　燒　魚
Spicy Deep-fried Fish

Catfish with Bean Paste Sauce

① { 1 catfish (about 1⅓-2 lbs.)
1 T. hot bean paste
1 T. each, chopped: green onions, ginger root, garlic

② { 1½ T. each: cooking wine, soy sauce
½ T. each: vinegar, sugar
½ t. salt
1½ c. water

③ { 1 T. cornstarch } mix
1 T. water
3 T. chopped onions
1 T. sesame oil
4 T. oil

❶ Clean the catfish and cut it in half; pat dry (see photo below).
❷ Heat the wok then add 4 T. oil. Fry the fish for 2 minutes or until both sides are golden brown; remove. Stir-fry ① until fragrant. Add the fish then ②; cover and cook over medium heat for 6 minutes or until the sauce reduced to half. Remove the fish and put in on a plate. Add ③ to thicken the remaining sauce; stir. Add green onions and sesame oil. Pour the liquid over the fish and serve.

■ Noodles or spaghetti may be added to mix with the sauce and served with the fish.

Spicy Deep-fried Fish

① { 1 rockfish or grouper (about 2 lbs.)
1 T. cooking wine
1 t. salt
oil

② { ½ c. chopped green onions
1 T. each: chopped ginger root, chopped garlic

③ { 3 T. ketchup
1 t. hot bean paste

④ { ¾ c. water
1 T. each: sugar, cooking wine, sesame oil
½ T. cornstarch
¾ t. salt

❶ Clean the fish and make a few deep cuts on the thick part of the fish. Marinate the fish in ① for 10 minutes. Combine ingredients ②, ③, and ④ in separate bowls.
❷ Heat the wok then add oil. Remove the fish and deep-fry it until golden brown; remove and put on a plate. Remove the oil.
❸ Heat the wok then add 4 T. oil. Stir-fry ② and ③ until fragrant. Add ④; stir until liquid thickens. Pour the liquid over the fish (see photo below) and serve hot.

> Any kind of fish may be used for the recipes on this page.

味 噌 燒 魚
Fish with Miso Sauce

紅 燒 魚
Fish Cooked in Soy Sauce

Fish with Miso Sauce

1   fish (about 1⅓ lbs.)

① {
3   T.   miso
2   T.   cooking wine
1   T.   soy sauce
½   T.   sugar
1   c.   water

4   T.   chopped green onions
½   T.   sesame oil
3   T.   oil

- Clean the fish and pat it dry. Heat the wok then add 3 T. oil. Fry the fish over high heat until both sides are golden brown. Add ① ; cover and bring to a boil. Cook over medium heat for 8 minutes or until the liquid is reduced to about ⅓ c. (turn the fish over during cooking). Sprinkle with green onions and sesame oil.
- ■ Miso (see photo below). Black bean paste or sweet bean paste may be substituted for miso, if miso is not available.

Fish Cooked in Soy Sauce

1   fish (about 1⅓ lbs.)

① {
1   T.   cooking wine
½   t.   salt

oil

② {
½   c.   green onions, 3 inches pieces
½   c.   shredded ginger root
1   hot pepper, cut lengthwise into 4 strips

③ {
4   T.   water
3   T.   soy sauce
2   T.   cooking wine
½   T.   sugar
1   t.   vinegar

- ❶ Clean the fish and pat it dry. Make a few deep cuts on the thick part of the fish. Marinate the fish with ① for at least 10 minutes; remove and pat dry.
- ❷ Heat the wok then add oil. Deep-fry the fish until golden brown (OR fry the fish until cooked); remove. Remove the oil.
- ❸ Heat the wok then add 2 T. oil. Stir-fry ② until fragrant. Add the fish and ③ bring to a boil. Turn the fish over and cook for 2 minutes.

三 杯 鯰 魚
Simmered Fish with
Bean Threads

三 杯 小 卷
Simmered Squid with
Bean Threads

Simmered Fish
with Bean Threads

```
    1    catfish (about 1⅓-2 lbs.)
         oil
    ½    T.  soy sauce
    4    T.  sesame oil
   ⎧6    slices ginger root
① ⎨8    cloves garlic, mashed
   ⎩1    dried hot pepper, cut into pieces
   ⎧½    c.  each: cooking wine, water
② ⎨¼    c.  soy sauce
   ⎩1    T.  sugar
    1    pkg   bean threads (1.5 oz.)
```

❶ Clean the fish and cut it into 1½ inches pieces. Mix the fish with ½ T. soy sauce (see photo below).

❷ Heat the wok then add oil. Deep-fry the fish until golden brown; remove. Remove the oil from the wok. Soak the bean threads in water until soft; remove and cut slightly.

❸ Heat the wok then add 4 T. sesame oil. Stir-fry ① until fragrant. Add the fish and ② . Cover and simmer over low heat for about 10 minutes. Add bean threads; cook for 5 minutes or until the liquid has almost evaporated. This dish is tastier when cooked in a Chinese clay pot. The Chinese clay is a casserole that may be used over a burner.

Simmered Squid
with Bean Threads

```
   1⅓  lbs. fresh squid
    ① and ② are the same as ingredients ① and ②
         of "Sirnmered Fish with Bean Threads"
         oil
    4    T.  sesame oil
    1    pkg. bean threads (1.5 oz.)
```

❶ Pull out the tentacles of the squid. Discard the eyes and the entrails of the body then cut the head into 4 pieces. Cut the body into rings, 1 inch wide.

❷ Other steps are the same as steps ❷ and ❸ of "Simmered Fish with Bean Threads". Coriander may be added, if desired.

Simmered Crab
with Bean Threads

```
    1    crab (about 2 lbs.)
    ingredients ① and ② are the same as ① and ②
         of "Simmered Fish with Bean Threads"
         oil
    4    T.  sesame oil
    1    pkg. bean threads (1.5 oz.)
```

❶ Clean the crab and cut it into large pieces.
❷ Other steps are the same as steps ❷ and ❸ of "Simmered Fish with Bean Threads".

紅 燒 鰻 魚
Eel Cooked in Soy Sauce

紅 燒 扣 鰻
Eel Steamed in
Soy Sauce

30

Eel Cooked in Soy Sauce

2 lbs. live eel
1½ T. cornstarch
oil
½ c. garlic cloves

① { 6 pieces green onions, 1 inch long
    6 slices ginger root
    6 Chinese black mushrooms, cut in half

② { 3 T. soy sauce
    1 T. each: cooking wine, sugar
    ½ T. sesame oil
    2 c. stock or water
    dash of pepper
    vinegar

③ { ½ T. cornstarch }
    { 1 T. water } mix

❶ Clean the eel and cut them into 1½ inch long pieces. Mix the eel with 1½ T. cornstarch.
❷ Heat the wok then add oil. Deep-fry the eel about 2 minutes or until golden brown; remove. Add garlic; deep-fry until golden brown. Remove the garlic then the oil.
❸ Heat the wok then add 3 T. oil. Stir-fry ① until fragrant. Add ②, garlic, eel and black mushrooms; cover and simmer for 20 minutes or until liquid is reduced to ⅓. Add ③ to thicken; stir. Serve.

> To prepare live eel; Cut off the head of the eel. When the eel stops moving; pour boiling water over it (Fig. 1). Remove any white membrane from the eel's skin (Fig. 2). Remove and discard entrails.

Eel steamed in Soy Sauce

Ingredients: See the ingredients of "Eel Cooked in Soy Sauce". Reduce the stock in ingredients ② to ½ c. Substitute bok choy for Chinese black mushroms and precook bok choy before using.

❶ See steps ❶ and ❷ of "Eel Simmered in Soy Sauce".
❷ Arrange the fried eel, cut side down, on a heatproof bowl. Add garlic and ②. Steam the eel for 40 minues. Pour the liquid into a saucepan. Place over medium heat; add ③ to thicken.
❸ Invert the heatproof bowl to a serving bowl. Arrange the bok choy around the eel. Pour the thickened liquid over the eel and bok choy.

Steamed Eel

2 live eel (about 1⅓ lbs.)

① { 6 pieces green onions, white part, 1 inch long
    4 slices ginger root

② { 5 c. water
    1 c. rice wine or cookig wine
    1¼ t. salt

❶ Clean the eel and cut them into 1½ inch lengths.
❷ Put ① in a heatproof bowl and add the eel and ②. Steam the eel for 1 hour. Remove and serve.

糟　溜　魚　片
Fish Fillets in Wine Sauce

檸　檬　魚　片
Fish Fillets in Lemon Sauce

Fish Fillets in Wine Sauce

⅔ lb. fish fillets (white meat)
① { ½ T. cooking wine
    ⅓ t. salt
    ½ egg white
    1 T. cornstarch
½ c. oil
② { 1 T. each: chopped green onions,
              chopped ginger root
    1½ T. rice wine or cooking wine
③ { ½ t. salt
    1 c. stock
    2 t. each: cornstarch, sugar

❶ Hold the knife at a 20° angle then cut the fish diagonaly into large, thin slices. Marinate it in ①. Mix the fish with 1 T. oil before frying so that the slices will separate easily during frying.

❷ Heat the wok then add oil. Add the fish; stir until cooked (precooking). Remove. Remove the oil. Reheat the wok; add 2 T. oil. Stir-fry ② until fragrant. Add ③ and bring it to a boil; add the fish and mix well. Remove and serve.

■ To make fermented rice (酒釀): Rinse 2C. steamed glutinous rice in cold water; drain and add ½C. granulated sugar. Disintegrate and sprinkle it. "酒麴" "chiu ch'ü" (fermenting yeast ball). See photo below. Mix the rice and fermenting yeast well; put it in an airtight container. Make an indentation in the rice to form a concave shape. Put the Container in a cool place and let stand for 4 days or until some liquid appears. Refrigerate the rice for 4 days; use. Fermented rice may be stored in the refrigerator for one month.

Fish Fillets in Lemon Sauce

⅔ lb. fish fillets
① { 1 T. cooking wine
    ⅓ t. salt
② { 2 eggs
    ½ c. each: flour, cornstarch
    ½ c. water
oil
③ { 5 T. lemon juice (or 4 T. vinegar)
    5 T. each: sugar, water
    ½ T. cornstarch
    ½ t. each: salt, sesame oil

❶ Hold the knife at a 20° angle then cut the fish into large, thin slices. Marinate them in ①. Mix ② into a batter.

❷ Heat the wok then add oil. Dip the fish in the batter then deep-fry it until golden brown and crispy; remove.

❸ Bring ③ to a boil; stir until it is thickened. Sprinkle over the fish and serve.

■ Lemon slices may be served with the fish and added as a garnish.

Sweet and Sour Fish Fillets

⅔ lb. fish fillets
① and ② are the same as ingredients ① and ② of "Fish Fillets in Lemon Sauce"
oil
½ onion, cut into pieces
③ { ½ green pepper, cut into pieces
    6 slices carrot
    6 straw mushrooms or button mushrooms
④ the same as ingredients ④ of "Fish Fillets in Lemon Sauce"

❶ See step ❶ and ❷ of "Fish Fillets in Lemon Sauce". Deep-fry the fish then remove it.

❷ Heat the wok then add 3 T. oil. Stir-fry onion until fragrant. Add ③; stir lightly. Add ④ and bring it to a boil; stir during cooking. Add the fish and mix well. Serve.

五 柳 魚
Fish with Five Vegetables

香 醋 燒 魚
Fish Cooked in Worcestershire Sauce

Fish with Five Vegetables

① { 1 whole fish about 1⅔ lbs.)
1 T. cooking wine
1 t. salt
2½ T. cornstarch
oil

② { ½ onion, shredded
1 T. dried shrimp,
   soak in water until soft before using
1 hot pepper, shredded

③ { 3 Chinese black mushrooms, shredded
⅓ c. each: shredded cucumber,
      shredded carrot
⅓ c. shredded meat, beef or pork

④ { 1¼ c. stock or water
1 T. vinegar
½ T. sugar
1¼ t. salt
dash of pepper
dash of sesame oil

⑤ { 1½ T. water
1 T. cornstarch } mix

❶ Clean the fish and pat it dry. Make deep cuts on the thick part of the fish. Marinate the fish in ① for at least 20 minutes. Remove and pat dry; coat with cornstarch.

❷ Heat the wok then add oil. Deep-fry the fish for 6 minutes or until golden brown and crispy; remove and put it on a serving plate.

❸ Heat the wok then add 3 T. oil. Stir-fry ② until fragrant. Add ③; stir lightly. Add ④ and bring to a boil. Add ⑤ to thicken; stir. Pour the mixture over the fish and serve.

Fish with Seven Vegetables

1 whole fish (about 1⅔ lbs.)
① the same as ingredients as ① of "Fish with Five Vegetables"
2½ T. cornstarch
oil

② { 6 pieces green onions, 1 inch long
6 slices ginger root

③ { Chinese black mushrooms
bamboo shoots, straw mushrooms,
green peas, carrot, lean meat } diced, combined to equal 1½ cups

④ the same as ingredients ④ of "Fish with Five Vegetables"

⑤ { 1½ T. water
1 T. cornstarch } mix

❶ See steps ❶ and ❷ of "Fish with Five Vegetables". Deep-fry the fish until golden brown; remove and put it on a serving plate.

❷ Heat the wok then add 3 T. oil. Stir-fry ② until fragrant. Add ③ and stir lightly. Add ④ and bring to a boil. Add ⑤ to thicken; stir. Pour the mixture over the fish and serve.

> Ingredients ③ may be substituted with green pepper, ham, canned baby corn, button mushrooms, etc.

Fish Cooked in Worcestershire Sauce

① { 1 whole fish (about 1⅔ lbs.)
1 T. cooking wine
1 t. salt
2 T. cornstarch
oil

3 oz. ground meat, pork or beef

② { 3 T. chopped green onions
½ T. each: chopped ginger root,
      chopped garlic
½ T. hot bean paste

③ { 1¼ c. water
2 T. each: soy sauce, Worcestershire sauce
1⅓ T. sugar
1 T. cooking wine
½ T. sesame oil

④ { 1 t. cornstarch
1 T. water } mix

2 T. chopped green onions

❶ Clean the fish. Make deep cuts on the thick part of the fish. Marinate the fish in ① for 20 minutes. Remove and pat it dry; coat with cornstarch.

❷ Heat the wok then add oil. Deep-fry the fish for 4 minutes or until golden brown; remove (or use 4 T. oil to fry fish until both sides are golden brown.) Remove the oil.

❸ Heat the wok then add 2 T. oil. Stir-fry ground meat until fragrant. Add ② and stir lightly (see photo below). Add ③ and the fish; cook for 5 minutes or until the liquid is reduced to half (turn the fish over during cooking.) Remove the fish and put it on a serving plate. Add ④ to the remaining liquid to thicken; stir. Pour the liquid over the fish. Sprinkle with green onions and serve.

紅 燒 魚 頭 (一)
Fish Head Cooked in
Soy Sauce (A)

Fish Head Steamed in Black Bean Sauce

1   fish head, select a large fleshy head (about 2 lbs.)

① {
2   T. each, chopped: Fermented black beans, ginger root
1   T. chopped garlic
1   hot pepper, sliced
2   T. each: soy sauce, cooking wine
1   T. each: sesame oil, cornstarch
½   t. salt
dash of pepper
}

- Clean the fish head and cut it into large pieces (see photo below). Marinate the fish in ① for 30 minutes. Steam the fish over boiling water, over high heat, for 15 minutes; remove and serve hot.

Fish Head Cooked in Soy Sauce (A)

1   large fish head (about 2 lbs.)
1   T. soy sauce
oil

① {
12   garlic clove
12   pieces green onions, 1 inch long
1   hot pepper
}

② {
3   T. each: soy sauce, cooking wine
1   T. each: vinegar, sugar, sesame oil
1¼   c. water
}

③ {
½   T. cornstarch
1   T. water
} mix

❶ Clean the fish head. Make deep cuts on the thick part of the fish. Rub 1 T. soy sauce evenly over the fish.

❷ Heat the wok then add oil. Deep-fry the fish head for 4 minutes or until golden brown; remove. (OR use 4 T. oil to fry the fish until both sides are golden brown.)

❸ Heat the wok then add 3 T. oil. Stir-fry ① until fragrant. Add the fish head and ② ; bring to a boil. Cover and simmer over low heat for 10 minutes or until liquid is reduced to half (turn the fish over during cooking). Add ③ to thicken; stir. Serve.

Fish Head Cooked in Soy Sauce (B)

- Ingredients and steps are the same as for "Fish Head Cooked in Soy Sauce (A)" except cut the fish head into pieces. Reduce the water in ingredients ② to 1 c. Shorten the simmering time of step ❸ to 5 minutes.

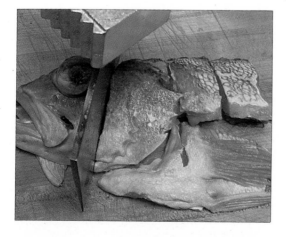

魚頭燒白菜
Stewed Fish Head with
Nappa Cabbage

砂鍋魚頭
Fish Head Casserole

38

Stewed Fish Head with Nappa Cabbage

    1   large fish head (about 2 lbs.)

① { 1½ T. soy sauce
     ½ T. cooking wine

      oil
    3   lbs. nappa cabbage, cut into pieces

② { 1½ T. soy sauce
     1½ t. salt
     1½ c. stock

❶ Clean the fish head and marinate it in ① for at least 10 minutes. Remove and pat dry; deep-fry or fry it until golden brown.

❷ Heat the wok then add 3 T. oil. Stir-fry the cabbage until it is soft. Transfer the cabbage to a casserole; put the fish in the center of the casserole. Add ② and stew over low heat for 1 hour.

> Fish head can either be deep-fried or fried, but deep-fried fish head tastes better.

Fish Head Casserole

    1   large fish head (about 2 lbs.)
    1   T. soy sauce • oil

① { ½ T. hot bean paste
     6   pieces green onions, 1 inch long
     6   slices ginger root • 6 garlic cloves

② { 12 slices each: lean meat (pork or chicken),
                   bamboo shoot
     6   Chinese black mushrooms, cut in half

③ { 5 T. soy sauce • 1 t. vinegar
     1 T. each: sugar, sesame oil • 2 c. stock
     1½ c. bean curd chunks

④ { 1 T. cornstarch } mix
     1 T. water

❶ Clean the fish head; cut it in half at the center (Fig. 1). Pat dry the fish and rub 1 T. soy sauce on it (Fig. 2).

❷ Heat the wok then add oil. Deep-fry the fish head for 3 minutes or fry it until golden brown; remove. Remove the oil.

❸ Heat the wok then add 3 T. oil. Deep-fry ① until fragrant. Add ② ; stir lightly. Add ③ and the fish; bring to a boil then reduce the heat. Cover and simmer over low heat for 10 minutes. Add bean curd and cook for 4 minutes. Add ④ to thicken; stir. Serve hot.

■ If a fresh fish head is used, step ❷ may be omitted. Fried fish head is very tasty. Other ingredients such as bok choy, nappa cabbage, bean thread sheets, bean threads, shrimp, fish balls, meat balls, sea cucumber, squid, etc. may be added to taste.

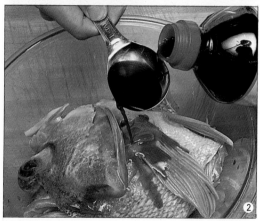

清 蒸 龍 利 魚
Steamed Flounder

乾 炸 龍 利 魚
Deep-fried Flounder

Steamed Flounder

1 flounder or sole (about 1⅔ lbs.)
① { 1 T. cooking wine
1 t. salt
② { 4 T. shredded green onions
2 T. coriander
dash of pepper
3 T. oil
③ { ½ c. stock or water
2 T. soy sauce
¼ t. salt

❶ Clean the fish then marinate it in ① for 20 minutes. Steam the fish, over boiling water, over high heat for 12 minutes or until cooked; remove the fish and discard the liquid. Sprinkle the fish with ② then drizzle with 3 T. boiling oil.
❷ Bring ③ to a boil; pour it over the fish. Serve.
■ Shredded hot pepper may be added to ingredients ②

> Besides flounder, rockfish, kingfish, or other kinds of fish may be used for cooking, frying or steaming. Fresh fish must be used when steaming.

Steamed American Shad

1 American shad (about 1⅓ lbs.)
① { 1 T. cooking wine
1 t. salt
½ c. diced meat or ground meat
② { 2 T. each, chopped: Chinese black mushrooms,
green onions
½ T. each, chopped: garlic, ginger root
1 hot pepper, sliced
③ { 1½ T. soy sauce
1 T. each: cooking wine, sesame oil

❶ Remove the entrails then clean the fish. Spread ① evenly over the fish and let it stand for 20minutes; remove and pat dry the fish. Put the fish on a heatproof plate.
❷ Mix the meat, ② and ③ thoroughly, spread this mixture on the fish. Steam the fish, over boiling water, over high heat for 12 minutes or until cooked.
■ OR stir-fry the meat, ② and ③ .spread the mixture on the fish then steam it. Sprinkle with shredded ginger root before serving. If desired, increase the soy sauce in the ingredients ③ to 1½ T. and reduce the salt in ingredients ① to ½ t.

Deep-Fried Flounder

1 flounder or sole (about 1⅔ lbs.)
① { 1 T. cooking wine
½ t. salt
oil
1½ T. chopped green onions
② { 1½ T. each: cooking wine, stock or water
¾ T. soy sauce

❶ Clean the fish; make deep cuts on the thick part of the body. Marinate the fish in ① for 20 minutes; remove and pat dry before deep-frying.
❷ Heat the wok then add the oil. Deep-fry the fish over high heat for 8 minutes or until golden brown and crispy; remove and put it on a plate. Remove the oil.
❸ Heat the wok then add 1 T. oil. Stir-fry the green onions until fragrant. Add ②; bring to a boil then drizzle it over the fish.
■ Other kind of fish may be substituted for flounder (see photo below)

Flounder and Green Onions Cooked in Soy Sauce

1 flounder or sole (about 1⅔ lbs.)
① { 1 T. cooking wine
½ t. salt
oil
12 pieces green onions, 6 inches long
② { 1 c. water
3 T. soy sauce
2 T. cooking wine
½ T. sesame oil
2 t. sugar
dash of pepper
③ { 1 t. cornstarch } mix
1 T. water

❶ Clean the fish then make deep cuts on the thick part of it. Cut the fish crosswise in half. Marinate the fish in ① for 10 minutes; remove and pat dry.
❷ Heat the wok then add oil. Deep-fry the green onions for 2 minutes; remove. Deep-fry the fish over high heat for 4 minutes or until golden brown (OR fry it until both sides are golden brown); remove. Remove the oil.
❸ Put ② in the wok then add green onions and fish; cover and cook over medium heat for 8 minutes or until the liquid is reduced to ⅓. Add mixture ③ to thicken; stir. Serve.

火 腿 蒸 魚
Steamed Fish with Ham

雪 菜 蒸 魚
Steamed Fish with
Salt Rape Greens

42

Steamed Fish with Ham

①
- 1 fish (about 1⅔ lbs.)
- 2 T. cooking wine
- ½ T. salt
- dash of pepper

- 6 slices ham
- 6 slices bamboo shoot

②
- ½ T. chopped green onions
- 1 t. sesame oil

● Clean the fish then marinate it in ① for 20 minutes. Arrange the slices of ham and bamboo shoot on the fish; steam them over high heat for 12 minutes or until fish is done. Sprinkle with ②.

Steamed Fish for Auspicious Presentation

- 1 fish (about 1⅔ lbs.)

①
- 1 T. cooking wine
- ½ t. salt
- ½ T. cornstarch

②
- 12 slices ham
- 12 slices each: bamboo shoot, Chinese black mushrooms
- 12 Chinese broccoli, 8 inches long
- 4 T. shredded green onions

③
- ¾ c. stock (include liquid from steaming fish)
- ½ T. cornstarch
- 1 t. cooking wine
- ½ t. salt
- dash of pepper

❶ Cut off the head and tail of the fish. Fillet the fish. Hold the knife at a 20° angle then cut the fish diagonally into 12 slices. Mix the sliced fish, head and tail with ① thoroughly. Coat the fish slices with ½ T. cornstarch.

❷ Arrange one slice of fish, bamboo shoot, Chinese black mushrooms, and ham as listed by overlapping them on a heatproof plate. Repeat the procedure until all the fish fillets and ② are arranged in two rows on the plate. Put the head and the tail on each side of the plate. Steam the fish, over boiling water, over high heat for 8 minutes or until the fish is cooked; remove.

❸ Remove and discard the wilted leaves of broccoli. Stir-fry the broccoli until it is done; arrange it around the fish. Arrange the shredded green onions lengthwise in the center of the plate. Bring ③ to a boil then pour it over the fish; serve.

■ The arrangement of this dish forms the "Chi Lin" shape, which is a fabulous animal resembling the deer and said to appear only in time of peace and prosperity. This dish is usually served at auspicious or happy occasions (such as weddings).

Steamed Fish with Salt Rape Greens

- 1⅓ lbs. fish

①
- 1 T. cooking wine
- 1 t. salt
- ⅔ c. chopped salt rape greens

②
- ⅓ c. shredded meat (beef or pork)
- 1 t. each: cornstarch, cooking wine
- 4 T. oil

③
- 1 hot red pepper, shredded
- ½ T. chopped garlic

④
- 1 T. soy sauce
- ½ T. sesame oil
- dash of pepper

❶ Clean the fish and cut it into steaks 1½ inches thick. Marinate the fish in ① for 20 minutes. Remove and pat dry; put the fish on a heatproof plate. Mix ② together.

❷ Heat the wok then add 4 T. oil. Stir-fry ② until the meat changes color; remove. Stir-fry ③ with the remaining oil until fragrant. Add salt rape greens; stir lightly. Add the meat and mix well; remove and put it on the fish. Sprinkle with ④. Steam the fish, over boiling water, over high heat for 12 minutes or until cooked. Serve.

■ Pickled mustard cabbage or pickled cucumber may be substituted for salt rape greens. If the pickled mustard cabbage is too salty, soak it in water for a few minutes then squeeze out the water before using.

> Any kind of fish may be used for steaming. Fresh fish is desirable. If the frozen fish is used, increase the steaming time.

Steamed Fish with Fermented Black Bean

- 1 fish (about 1⅓ lbs.)
- ① the same as ingredients ① of "Steamed Fish with Salt Rape Greens"
- 2½ oz. ground meat

①
- 1½ T. fermented black beans
- ½ T. chopped garlic
- 1 hot pepper, sliced

- 1 T. oil

②
- 2½ T. soy sauce
- 1 T. cooking wine
- 1 t. sesame oil
- 2 T. shredded ginger root

❶ Clean the fish and marinate it in ① for 20 minutes.

❷ Heat the wok then add 1 T. oil. Stir-fry ② until fragrant. Add the meat; stir until cooked. Add ③ and stir lightly; remove and spread over the fish. Steam the fish, over boiling water, over high heat for 12 minutes or until it is cooked; remove. For added flavor, sprinkle with 2 T. shredded ginger root before serving.

烤 蛤 蜊
Baked Clams

烤大草蝦
Baked Prawns

Baked Clams

12 large clams
salt

❶ Release the sand from the clams (see p. 11 for preparing clams). Scrub the shells and clean them. Cut off the joint of the shells (see photo below) to prevent the shells from opening. This keeps the juice from escaping during baking.

❷ Spread water then salt on both shells of the clams. Preheat the oven to 500°F. Bake the clams for 5 minutes or put the clams on a rack then bake them on the stove.

Baked Prawns

12 prawns (about 1 lb.)
1 T. cooking wine
1 t. salt
4 wooden or steel skewers, 6 inches long
½ lemon, sliced

❶ Devein and clean the prawns. Insert a skewer through the heads of 6 prawns and insert another skewer through the tails of the 6 prawns. Use the same procedure for the remaining 6 prawns (see photo below). Sprinkle wine then salt on the prawns.

❷ Preheat the oven to 550°F. Bake the prawns on the middle rack for 8 minutes or until cooked. Sprinkle with lemon juice before serving, if desired.

■ Sprinkling wine on the prawns helps keep the salt on the prawns. This also makes the prawns more attractive and better tasting.

百角蝦丸
Shrimp Balls with
Diced Bread

炸鑲蟹鉗
Crabs Claws in
Shrimp Balls

Shrimp Balls
with Diced Bread

⅔ lb. shrimp paste
1 c. coarsely diced, stale bread
oil
dipping sauce: Szechuan peppercorn salt or
ketchup

❶ Arrange the bread on a plate. Form the shrimp
paste into 12 balls then coat them with the
diced bread.

❷ Heat the wok then add oil. Deep-fry the shrimp
balls over medium heat for 3 minutes or until
golden brown. If necessary, adjust the heat
during frying. If the heat is too low, the bread will
fall off. If the heat is too high, the bread will burn.

■ To make shrimp paste: Clean ⅔ lb. shrimp then
mash them with a meat mallet or a mixer, the
finer the better. Add 1 T. cooking wine, ½ t. finely
grated ginger root, ½ t. salt, 1 egg white, and 1 T.
cornstarch to the shrimp; mix thoroughly.

Cuttlefish Balls

● Ingredients and steps are the same as for shrimp
paste, except substitute cuttlefish or squid for
shrimp to make cuttlefish balls or squid balls.
Deep-fry or cook the balls in water.

Crabs Claws
in Shrimp Balls

12 frozen crabs claws
① 1 T. cooking wine
⅓ t. salt
2 green onions
2 slices ginger root
⅔ lb. shrimp paste
1 c. bread crumbs
oil
dipping sauce: Szechuan peppercorn salt or
ketchup

❶ Clean the claws then mix them with ①. Steam
the crabs claws over boiling water, over high
heat, for 5 minutes; remove and let cool.

❷ Put the bread crumbs on a plate. Form the
shrimp paste into 12 balls then put them on the
plate. Insert a claw into each shrimp ball (Fig. 1).
Coat the shrimp balls with bread crumbs (Fig. 2).

❸ Heat the wok then add oil. Deep-fry the shrimp
balls over medium heat for 4 minutes or until
they are golden brown and have expanded
slightly. Serve with dipping sauce.

■ Diced: Chinese black mushrooms, carrot, bamboo shoots or water chestnuts may be added to
the shrimp paste, if desired.

炸百花蝦
Deep-fried Shrimp with
Assorted Vegetables

蝦仁豆腐
Shrimp with Bean Curd

Deep-fried Shrimp with Assorted Vegetables

18 medium shrimp

① { ½ T. cooking wine
    ¼ t. salt
    dash of pepper

② { green pepper, carrot, green onions, Chinese black mushrooms } chopped and combined into equal 1½ cups

③ { 1 egg
    ¾ c. water
    2 t. sugar
    ¼ t. salt
    1 c. flour
    oil

❶ Shell the shrimp and leave the tail intact. Devein the shrimp; clean and drain them. Score the belly of the shrimp to prevent them from curling during deep-frying. Add ① to the shrimp and mix thoroughly.

❷ Mix ③ thoroughly. Add ② and flour (Fig. 1); mix to form a flour batter.

❸ Heat the wok then add oil. Dip the shrimp in the flour batter; remove it with a spoon (Fig. 2). Deep-fry the shrimp for 4 minutes or until golden brown; remove. Serve with ketchup, mayonnaise or Szechuan peppercorn salt.

■ Ingredients ② may be varied, if desired.

Shrimp with Bean Curd

¼ lb. shrimp

① { 1 t. cooking wine
    1/6 t. salt
    ½ T. cornstarch

3 T. oil
6 pieces green onions, 1 inch long
6 slices ginger root

② { 1½ c. stock or water
    1¼ t. each: salt, sugar
    dash of pepper

③ { 2 c. bean curd chunks, 1 inch square
    1 tomato, diced
    ⅓ c. each: button mushrooms or straw mushrooms, green peas

④ { 1½ T. cornstarch
    2 T. water } mix
½ T. sesame oil

❶ Clean the shrimp (see p. 12). Add ① ; mix well.

❷ Heat the wok then add 3 T. oil. Stir-fry the shrimp until cooked; remove. Use the remaining oil to stir-fry green onions and ginger root until fragrant. Add ② ; bring to a boil. Add ③ ; bring to a boil. Cook for 2 minutes. Add the shrimp then mixture ④ to thicken; stir. Add sesame oil.

■ Ingredients ③ may be varied, if desired.

燒酒草蝦
Prawns Cooked in Wine

蛋黃大蝦
Prawns-Egg Rolls

Prawns Cooked in Wine

        12   prawns (about ¾-1 lb.)
      ⎧ 1   c. each: rice wine or cooking wine, water
  ① ⎨ ½   t. salt
      ⎩ 6   slices ginger root

❶ Devein the prawns; wash and drain them.
❷ Bring ① to a boil then reduce the heat to low;
   continue to cook for 5 minutes. Add the prawns
   then cook for 2 minutes or until they are cooked.
   The soup in this dish is very delicious. The prawns
   may be served alone or with the soup.
■ This dish is especially delicious if live prawns are
   used. Crab and chicken may be cooked in the
   same method.

Prawns-Egg Rolls

        6   prawns
      ⎧ 1   t. cooking wine
  ① ⎨ 1/6 t. salt
      ⎩ dash of pepper
        cornstarch
      ⎧ 1   egg
  ② ⎨ 4   T. cornstarch
        6   salty egg yolks
        6   pieces nori, 1"x2"
        oil

❶ Shell the prawns and leave the tails intact.
   Devein the prawns; wash and drain them. Cut
   lengthwise at the back of each prawn to open
   it. Marinate the prawns in ① for 10 minutes;
   sprinkle with cornstarch then flatten them with a
   meat mallet (Fig. 1). Mix ② well. Put a salty egg
   yolk on a nori then roll it up jelly-roll style. Use the
   same method to make the other 5 rolls.
❷ Put 3 T. cornstarch on a plate. Dip a prawn in
   mixture ② then put it, cut side up, on the
   cornstarch. Put a roll on the prawn; roll up the
   prawn jelly-roll style (Fig. 2). Coat the prawn with
   cornstarch. Follow the same procedures for the
   other 5 prawns.
❸ Heat the wok then add oil. Deep-fry the prawns
   for 5 minutes or until golden brown and crispy;
   remove. Cut the prawns in half then serve.

紫菜蝦腿
Shirmp-Nori Rolls

乾煎蝦
Fried Shrimp

Shrimp-Nori Rolls

24	shrimp in shell

① | ½ | T. cooking wine |
| ¼ | t. salt |

② | ½ | lb. shrimp, shelled |
| 2 | green onions |
| ⅓ | c. water chestnuts or onions |

③ | ½ | t. salt |
2	t. sugar
2	t. cornstarch
	dash of sesame oil

6	nori sheets, 8" x 8"
3	T. flour
4	T. water
	oil

❶ Shell the shrimp and leave the tails intact. Clean the shrimp then pat them dry. Marinate the shrimp in ① for 10 minutes.

❷ To prepare the filling: Chop ② and mix it with ③. Divide the mixture into 24 portions.

❸ Cut each nori in quarters. Mix the flour and the water to form a paste.

❹ Spread some flour paste on the edges of a nori. Put a portion of the filling on the center of the nori (◇) then put a shrimp on the top of the filling; leave the tail outside the nori. Fold the nori to form a triangle; leave the tail unwrapped. Follow the same procedure to make the other 23 rolls.

❺ Heat the wok then add oil. Deep-fry the shrimp over medium heat for 2 minutes; turn the heat to high and continue deep-frying for 1 minute. Remove. Serve with Szechuan peppercorn salt or ketchup.

Deep-fried Prawns with Bread

12	prawns in shell (about 1⅓ lbs.)

① | ½ | T. cooking wine |
| ½ | t. salt |

② | 3 | T. flour |
| 1 | T. cornstarch |

6	slices bread
4	egg white
	oil
1	t. chopped ham
½	t. black sesame seeds
24	leaves of coriander

❶ Shell and remove the head of the prawns, leave the tails intact. Make a cut at the back of each prawn to butterfly. Devein the prawns then flaten them lightly with the flat side of a cleaver. Marinate the prawns with ① for 10 minutes.

❷ Cut off the crust from the slices of bread; halve each slice. Beat the egg whites until stiff peaks form (about 8 minutes). Add ② ; mix well to form a batter.

❸ Pat dry the prawns. Spread some batter over each bread. Put the prawns, back side down, on the pieces of bread. Spread the remaining batter evenly over the prawns and the bread. Garnish with ham, coriander and sesame seeds.

❹ Heat the wok then add oil. Deep-fry the prawns, prawn side down, over low heat, until they are done. Turn the prawns over and continue deep-frying. Turn the heat to high before removing them. Total deep-frying time is about 6 minutes.

Fried Shrimp

18	medium shrimp

① | ½ | T. cooking wine |
| ⅙ | t. salt |

② | 2 | egg yolks |
½	T. water
1¼	T. flour
⅛	t. salt

③ | 1 | T. each: coriander (or chopped onion), chopped ham (or chopped hot pepper) |
	dash of pepper
	cornstarch
2	T. oil

❶ Wash and drain the shrimp. Make a cut at the back of each shrimp to butterfly. Devein the shrimp. Score the inside surface of the shrimp to prevent them from curling during frying. Marinate the shrimp in ① for 10 minutes. Mix ② together.

❷ Sprinkle the inside surface of the shrimp with cornstarch then spread with ②. Garnish with ③ (Fig. 1).

❸ Heat the pan then add 2 T. oil. Place the shrimp, shell side down, in the pan. Fry the shrimp over medium heat for 1 minute (Fig. 2); cover and cook until done (about 2 minutes).

彩色蝦仁
Stir-fried Shrimp wit
Assorted Vegetable

鼓汁蝦球
Stir-fried Shrimp with
Black Beans

56

Stir-fried Shrimp with Assorted Vegetables

½ lb. shrimp, shelled
① { ¼ t. salt
    ¾ T. cooking wine
    ¾ T. cornstarch
½ c. oil
6 pieces green onions, 1 inch long
1 c. peeled, diced cucumber
¾ c. whole canned corn kernels
② { 2 T. water
    1 t. cornstarch
    ⅓ t. each: cooking wine, salt, sesame oil
    dash of pepper

❶ Clean and wash the shrimp (see p. 12); pat them dry. Add ① to the shrimp; stir to mix. Add 1 T. oil and mix well before frying so that the shrimp will separate easily during frying. Mix ② in a bowl.

❷ Heat the wok then add oil. Stir-fry the shrimp until cooked (precooking); remove. Remove the oil. Reheat the wok then add 2 T. oil. Stir-fry the green onions until fragrant. Add cucumber; stir for 1 minute. Add corn and stir lightly. Add shrimp and ② ; stir quickly over high heat until mixed well. Remove and serve.

■ Carrot, bamboo shoot, onion, or green peas may be substituted for cucumber and corn.

■ Stir-fried shrimp may be served in a bird's nest made of potato, taro root, or noodles for an elegant presentation (see photo below). To make bird's nest see p. 91, "Seafood in Potato Bird's Nest".

Stir-fried Shrimp with Black Beans

¾ lb. shrimp, shelled
① { ½ t. salt
    1 T. cooking wine
    1 T. cornstarch
½ c. oil
② { ½ T. fermented black beans, cut through lightly
    1 t. each: chopped garlic, chopped hot pepper
    12 pieces green onions, 1 inch long
③ { 1½ T. water
    1 T. soy sauce
    ⅔ t. cornstarch

❶ Make a cut at the back of each shrimp to butterfly them. Clean and wash the shrimp then pat them dry. Add ① to the shrimp; stir to mix. Add 1 T. oil and mix well before frying so that the shrimp will separate easily during frying. Mix ③ in a bowl.

❷ Heat the wok then add oil. Stir-fry the shrimp until cooked (precooking); remove. Remove the oil. Heat the wok then add 1 T. oil. Stir-fry ② until fragrant. Add the shrimp and ③; stir quickly over high heat until mixed well.

■ Fermented black beans are black beans that have been steamed, fermented and marinated in salty water then allowed to dry. It is better to rinse fermented black beans before using (see photo below).

滑 蛋 蝦 仁
Stir-fried Shrimp with Eggs

宮 保 蝦 仁
Stir-fried Shrimp
with Dried Hot Peppe

Stir-fried Shrimp with Eggs

- ⅓ lb. shrimp, shelled
- ① { 1/6 t. salt
     ½ T. each: cooking wine, cornstarch
- ② { ¼ c. sliced button mushrooms or straw mushrooms
     ¼ c. green peas or chopped green onions
- 5 eggs
- ③ { ½ T. cooking wine
     ½ t. salt
     dash of pepper
- 7 T. oil

❶ Clean; wash and drain the shrimp (see p. 12). Add ① to the shrimp; mix. Beat the eggs; add ③ and mix well.

❷ Heat the wok then add 4 T. oil. Stir-fry the shrimp until cooked; remove. Stir-fry ② until cooked; remove. Heat the wok then add 3 T. oil. Add the egg, the shrimp, and ②; rotate the wok until the egg is slightly solid; remove and serve.

Stir-fried Shrimp with Asparagus

- ½ lb. shrimp, shelled
- ① { ¼ t. salt
     ¾ T. each: cooking wine, cornstarch
- ½ c. oil
- ⅔ lb. fresh asparagus
- ½ c. button mushrooms or straw mushrooms
- ② { 6 pieces green onions, 1 inch long
     6 slices ginger root
     ½ T. chopped garlic
- ③ { 2 T. water
     1 t. each: cornstarch, sesame oil
     ⅓ t. salt
     dash of pepper
- 1 T. wine

❶ Clean, wash and drain the shrimp (see p. 12). Cut large shrimp in half lengthwise at the back. Marinate the shrimp in ① for 10 minutes.

❷ Cut off any hard stalks and wilted skin of the asparagus. Clean the asparagus then cut them into 3 inch lengths. Cut the mushrooms in half.

❸ Heat the wok then add oil. Stir-fry the shrimp until cooked; remove. Remove the oil and reheat the wok then add 2 T. oil. Stir-fry ② until fragrant. Add the asparagus, mushrooms and 1 T. wine; stir-fry for 2 minutes. Add the shrimp and ③; stir quickly until mixed well.

Stir-fried Shrimp with Dried Hot Pepper

- ⅔ lb. shrimp, shelled
- ① { ½ t. salt
     1 T. each: cooking wine, egg white, cornstarch oil
- ② { 3 dried hot pepper, cut into pieces, seeds removed (see photo below)
     10 pieces green onions, 1 inch long
- 1 green pepper, cut into pieces
- ½ c. fried cashews or fried peanuts
- ③ { 1½ T. water
     1½ T. soy sauce
     ½ T. cooking wine
     2 t. sugar
     1 t. each: vinegar, cornstarch

❶ Clean, wash and drain the shrimp (see p. 12); mix thoroughly with ①

❷ Heat the wok then add oil. Stir-fry the shrimp until cooked (precooking); remove. Remove the oil.

❸ Heat the wok then add 2 T. oil. Stir-fry ② until fragrant. Add green peppers; stir lightly. Add the shrimp and ③; stir quickly until mixed well. Sprinkle with cashews or peanuts; remove. Serve.

清 蒸 草 蝦
Steamed Prawns

怪 味 蝦 球
Prawns with Hot Sauce

Steamed Prawns

12 prawns in shell (about ¾ lb.)

① { 1 T. cooking wine
¼ t. salt
2 green onions
2 slices ginger root }

② { 1 T. mustard
2 T. water
1 T. soy sauce } dipping sauce

❶ Mix ② thoroughly. Keep it in an airtight container until ready to use. To make dipping sauce, add soy sauce to ② when ready to use.

❷ Devein and clean the prawns. Marinate the prawns in ① for 10 minutes. Steam the prawns over boiling water, over high heat, for 4 minutes. Turn off the heat and let stand for 2 minutes; remove. Serve with dipping sauce after removing the shells.

■ To prevent the prawns from curling during steaming, thread a skewer through the head of each prawn and thread another skewer through the tail of each prawn before steaming (see p. 45, photo of "Baked Prawns").

Shrimp Cooked in Salty Water

⅔ lb. fresh shrimp

① { 2 c. water
2 T. cooking wine
½ T. salt
2 green onions
2 slices ginger root }

② { 1 T. mustard
2 T. water
1 T. soy sauce } dipping sauce

❶ Mix ② thoroughly. Keep it in an airtight container until ready to use. To make dipping sauce, add soy sauce to ② when ready to use.

❷ Clean the shrimp. Bring ① to a boil. Add the shrimp and bring to a boil again; turn off the heat and let stand for 2 minutes. Remove. Serve with dipping sauce after removing the shells.

Prawns with Hot Sauce

⅔ lb. prawn

① { 2 c. water
2 T. cooking wine
½ T. salt
2 green onions
2 slices ginger root }

1 c. sliced cucumber or lettuce
1 c. presoaked bean thread sheet

② { 1 T. peanut butter or sesame paste
3 T. soy sauce
⅔ T. each: sugar, vinegar
2 T. chopped green onions
½ T. each: chopped garlic, chili oil }

❶ Shell, devein and clean the prawns. Make three cuts lengthwise at the back of each prawn; do not cut through (Fig. 1) OR cut each prawn in half then make a cut lengthwise on each half; do not cut through (Fig. 2).

❷ Soak the cucumber in ice water for 5 minutes; drain then arrange it in a circle on a serving plate. Put the bean thread sheets in the center of the plate.

❸ Bring ① to a boil. Add the prawns and bring to a boil. Remove, drain and put them on the bean thread sheets.

■ If small shrimp are used, cook the shrimp in shell in ① until cooked. Shell the shrimp and serve them wth ② or mustard sauce.

■ Bean thread sheets may be omitted if they are not available.

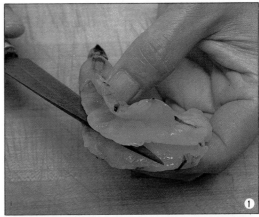

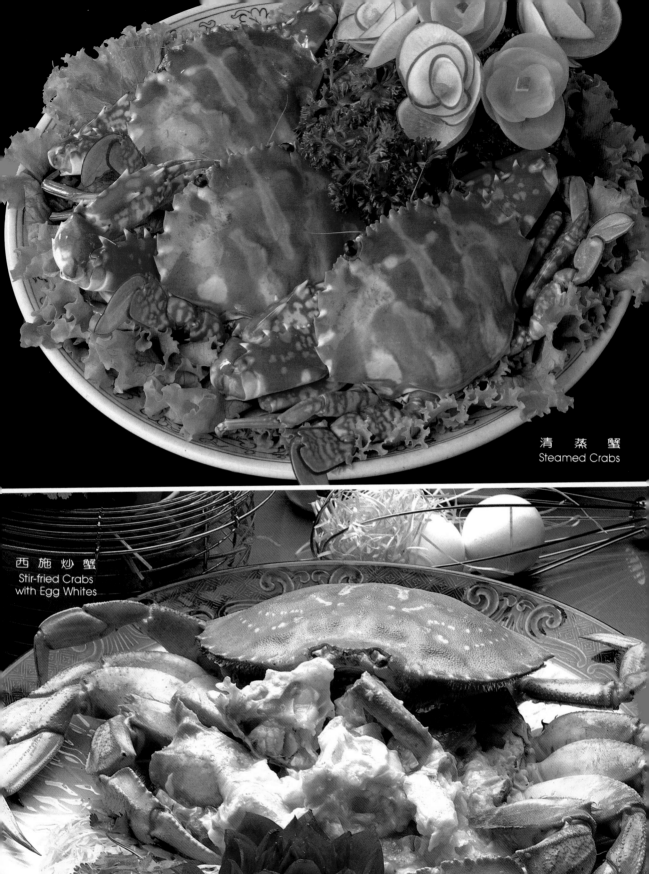

清　蒸　蟹
Steamed Crabs

西施炒蟹
Stir-fried Crabs
with Egg Whites

Steamed Crabs

	2	crabs, live in shell (about 2 lbs.)
①	⎰ 2	whole green onions
	⎱ 2	slices ginger root
	1	T. cooking wine
	1	t. salt
	⎰ 3	T. vinegar
②	⎱ ½	t. salt
	1½	T. chopped ginger root

- Clean the crabs (see p. 11). Add ① to the crabs, steam over high heat for 15 minutes. Cut the crabs into pieces and arrange them on a serving plate; serve with ②
- Any kind of crab may be used in this recipe. To arrange the crab on the serving plate, see photo below.
- To simplify procedures for family use: Clean the crabs then place them with ① and 1 c. water in a pot. Cover the pot; cook the crabs for 10 minutes. Remove the crabs and serve with ②

Stir-fried Crabs with Egg Whites

2	lbs. crabs
3	T. oil
① ⎰ 1	T. chopped green onions
⎱ ½	T. chopped ginger root
② ⎰ 1	c. stock
⎰ 1	T. cooking wine
⎱ 1	t. salt
③ ⎰ 1	t. cornstarch
⎱ 1	T. water
4	egg whites, beaten

- Clean the crabs then cut them into pieces (see p. 11). Heat the wok then add 3 T. oil. Stir-fry ① until fragrant; add ② and the crabs. Cover and cook for 6 minutes. Remove the legs, claws and shells and arrange them on a serving plate. Add ③ to the remaining ingredients; stir to thicken. Add egg whites then stir-fry over low heat until the egg becomes solid. Put the mixture over the crab pieces and serve.

Stir-fried Crabs with Eggs

2	lbs. crabs, live in shell
① ⎰ 1	T. cooking wine
⎱ ⅓	t. salt
2	T. cornstarch
	oil

② ⎰ yellow Chinese chives or bamboo shoot / carrot / Chinese black mushrooms / onion ⎱ — shredded and combined to equal 2 cups

③ ⎰ 4 eggs / ¾ t. salt / dash of pepper / dash of sesame oil ⎱ — mix

❶ Clean the crabs then cut them into pieces (see p. 11). Marinate in ① for 10 minutes. Drain the crab before deep-frying. Coat them with cornstarch.

❷ Heat the wok then add oil. Deep-fry the crabs until golden brown; remove. Remove the oil.

❸ Heat the wok; add 3 T. oil. Stir-fry the onions in ② until fragrant; add the remaining ingredients in ② and stir lightly. Add ③ and crabs; stir-fry until the egg is golden brown or slightly solid. Remove and serve.

葱　油　蟹
Steamed Crabs with Green Onions

葱　爆　蟹
Stir-fried Crabs with Green Onions

Steamed Crabs with Green Onions

1½ lbs. crabs
① {
1 whole hot pepper, shredded
4 T. shredded green onions
2 T. shredded ginger root
}
dash of pepper
1 t. soy sauce
② {
½ c. stock or water
1 t. sesame oil
¾ t. salt
}

- Clean the crabs. Steam the crabs over boiling water, over high heat, for 12 minutes; remove and cut them into pieces. Put the pieces of crab on a serving plate and arrange ① on top of the crab. Bring ② to a boil; pour it over the crab and ① . Serve.

Stir-fried Crabs with Fermented Black Beans

1½-2 lbs. crabs
3 T. oil
½ c. coarsely diced onions
① {
2 T. fermented black beans
1 T. minced garlic
}
② {
1¼ c. stock or water
2 T. each: cooking wine, soy sauce
1 t. each: sesame oil, sugar
}
③ {
2 t. cornstarch
1½ T. water
} mix

❶ Clean the crabs then cut them into pieces (see p. 11).
❷ Heat the wok then add 3 T. oil. Stir-fry the onions until fragrant. Add ① and the crabs; stir lightly. Add ② and cover the wok; cook for 5 minutes or until the liquid is reduced to half. Add ③ to thicken and stir; serve.

Stir-fried Crabs with Green Onions

1½-2lbs. crabs
12 whole green onions
3 T. oil
① {
1 c. stock or water
2 T. cooking wine
1 T. each: soy sauce, oyster sauce
¼ t. salt
}
dash of pepper
② {
1 T. cornstarch
1½ T. water
} mix
½ T. sesame oil

❶ Clean the crabs then cut them into pieces (see p. 11). Cut the green onions into 4 inch lengths; separate the white part and green part.
❷ Heat the wok then add 3 T. oil. Stir-fry the white part of the onions until fragrant. Add the crabs and stir lightly. Add ① ; cover and cook over high heat for 5 minutes or until the liquid is reduced to half. Add the green part of the onions. Add ② to thicken; stir. Sprinkle with sesame oil; serve.

蟹 肉 菜 圓
Crab Meat with Vegetable Balls

Crab Meat with Vegetable Balls

① {
white radish
carrot
cucumber
straw mushrooms or button mushrooms
} scooped-out balls } combined to equal 4 cups

② {
2   c. stock
½   T. cooking wine
¾   t. salt
½   t. sugar
dash of pepper
}
½ c. crab meat

③ {
1   T. cornstarch
2   T. water
} mix

● Cook ① and ② in a wok or pan for 15 minutes. Add crab meat; add ③ to thicken the liquid. Stir gently and serve.

Crab Meat with Yellow Chinese Chives

⅔   lb. yellow Chinese chives
2   T. oil
⅓   lb. crab meat (about 1 c.)

① {
1   c. stock
1   T. cooking wine
½   t. salt
dash of sesame oil
dash of pepper
}

② {
1   T. cornstarch
2   T. water
} mix

❶ Remove any wilted leaves from the chives. Cut the chives into 2 inch lengths. Heat the wok then add 2 T. oil. Stir-fry the chives quickly over high heat; remove and put them on a serving plate.

❷ Bring ① to a boil. Add crab meat and ② to thicken; stir. Pour the mixture over the chives and serve (Fig. 1).

Crab Meat with Bok Choy

½   c. crab meat
1⅓ lbs. bok choy
3   T. oil
6   green onions, 1 inch long

① {
1½ c. stock
½   T. cooking wine
¾   t. salt
dash of pepper
dash of sesame oil
}

② {
1½ T. cornstarch
2   T. water
} mix

❶ Remove any wilted leaves from the bok choy. Lengthwise halve or quarter large bok choy. Plunge the bok choy in boiling water; remove. Rinse the bok choy in cold water; drain.

❷ Heat the wok then add 3 T. oil. Stir-fry green onions until fragrant. Add the bok choy; stir lightly. Add ① , cook until the bok choy is tender. Add crab meat and ② to thicken; stir gently and serve (Fig. 2).

■ Celery, nappa cabbage or cucumber may be substituted for bok choy. Scallops may be substituted for crab meat.

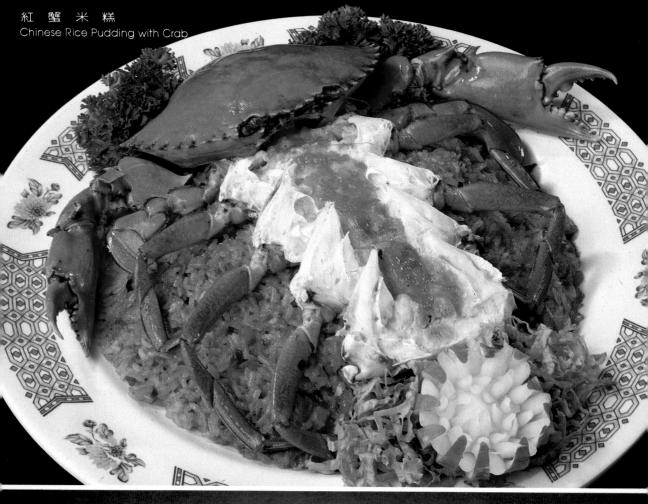

紅　蟹　米　糕
Chinese Rice Pudding with Crab

海　鮮　鍋　飯
Rice and Seafood

Chinese Rice Pudding with Crab

1 crab (about 2 lbs.)
2 c. glutinous rice
3 T. oil

① {
½ c. diced lean meat, beef or pork
¼ c. diced Chinese black mushrooms
2 T. dried shrimp
}

② {
2 T. soy sauce
1 T. cooking wine
2 t. each: sesame oil, sugar
¼ t. salt
dash of pepper
}

❶ Heat the wok then add 3 T. oil. Stir-fry ① until it is cooked. Add ② and stir lightly; remove.

❷ Rinse the rice. Cook the rice in 1½ c. water. Mix the rice with ② while it is hot.

❸ Clean the crab and cut it into pieces. Arrange the crab on the rice; steam over high heat until the crab is cooked. Serve.

Rice and Seafood

3 c. rice

① {
3 c. water
2 T. each: soy sauce, cooking wine
½ T. sesame oil
½ t. each: salt, sugar
dash of pepper
}

② {
1 dried, medium squid
12 shrimp
⅓ lb. oysters
½ c. lean pork or ham
2 T. dried shrimp
}

③ {
¾ c. diced carrots, ⅓ inch cubes
¾ c. mushrooms or bamboo shoots, cut into ⅓ inch cubes
½ c. grean peas
}

❶ Cut the squid into pieces, 1½ inches long, 1 inch wide. Devein shrimp. Cut the pork into ⅓ inch cubes. Soak the dried shrimp in water. Cut large oysters in half. Rinse rice and drain.

❷ Mix rice, ①, ②, and ③ together well. Cook the rice in a rice cooker (see photo below). Serve hot.

■ A pot may be used to substitute for rice cooker. If a pot is used, soak the rice in ① for 30 minutes then mix with ② and ③. Bring the liquid to a boil; continue to cook over high heat for 1 minute. Cover the pot and simmer the rice over low heat for 30 minutes. Turn off the heat; keep the pot covered for 10 minutes. Serve.

■ Ingredients ② may be substituted with scallops, crabs, squid, clams, fish, sea cucember, fish fin, etc.

生菜鮑魚
Stir-fried Abalone
with Lettuce

奶汁鮑魚
Creamy Abalone

Stir-fried Abalone with Lettuce

1 c. sliced abalone
1½ c. or 1 can straw mushrooms
1 lb. lettuce
2. T. oil
6 pieces green onions, 1 inch long
6 slices ginger root

① { 6 T. stock
    1⅓ T. each: oyster sauce, soy sauce
    1 t. cornstarch
    1 t. each: sesame oil, sugar

❶ Cut the mushrooms in half. Blanch the lettuce leaves in boiling water; remove and drain. Put the lettuce on a serving plate.

❷ Heat the wok then add 2 T. oil. Stir-fry the green onions and ginger root until fragrant. Add the mushrooms and stir lightly. Add the abalone and ① ; stir quickly over high heat. Put the abalone over the lettuce and serve.

■ If live abalone is used, pry the whole foot muscle from the shell (Fig. 1); remove and discard the stomach. Clean the abalone then slice it (Fig. 2). Mix the abalone with 1 T. cornstarch. Precook the abalone in ½ c. oil before stir-frying it.

■ Live abalone may be served raw. Slice the abalone then refrigerate it. Serve the abalone with dipping sauce (see p. 95, "Raw Lobster with Mustard Sauce").

Creamy Abalone

½ can abalone
4 T. oil
½ c. chopped onions
2½ T. flour

① { ¾ c. stock
    ¼ c. liquid of canned abalone
    ¾ t. salt
    dash of pepper

② { ½ c. each: carrot, cauliflower; cut into pieces
    ½ c. mushrooms
    3 whole bok choy, cut in half
    ¼ c. evaporated milk (or ½ c. milk)

❶ Cut the abalone into thin slices. Heat the wok then add 4 T. oil. Stir-fry the onions until fragrant. Add flour and stir lightly over low heat until the flour is slightly brown and forms a paste.

❷ Bring ① to a boil. Add ② and cook for 5 minutes; add the abalone and milk. Add the flour paste to thicken. Serve.

乾 燒 生 蠔
Spicy Deep-fried Oysters

檸 汁 生 蠔
Oysters in Lemon Sauce

Spicy Deep-fried Oysters

① { ⅔ lb. shucked oysters
1/6 t. salt
dash of pepper
1 T. flour
oil

② { ¾ c. flour
½ t. baking powder
⅓ c. water
1 egg
¼ t. salt

③ { 3 T. chopped green onions
1 T. chopped garlic
½ T. chopped ginger root
3 T. ketchup
1 t. chili paste

④ { 1 T. each: cooking wine, sugar
½ T. each: sesame oil, cornstarch
¾ t. salt
1 c. stock or water

❶ Clean the oysters and cut the large oysters in half. Cook the oysters in boiling water for 1 minute; remove and drain. Add ① to the oysters and mix well. Mix ② into a paste.

❷ Heat the wok then add oil. Coat the oysters with mixture ② then deep-fry it for 3 minutes or until golden brown; remove. Remove the oil.

❸ Heat the wok; add 3 T. oil. Stir-fry ③ until fragrant then add ④. Bring to a boil and cook until the liquid is thickened. Transfer the liquid to a serving plate and place the oysters on it; serve.

Crispy Deep-fried Oysters

● See steps ❶ and ❷ of "Spicy Deep-fried Oysters". Serve the oysters with Szechuan peppercorn salt or ketchup.

Oysters with Fermented Black Beans

1 lb. shucked oysters
1 t. salt
3 T. oil

① { 3 T. fermented black beans
1 T. chopped garlic
½ T. chopped ginger root
1 red pepper, sliced
1 c. chopped green onions

② { 2½ T. soy sauce
1 T. water
½ T. sesame oil
1 t. cornstarch

❶ Mix the oysters with 1 t. salt; rinse and drain. Cut large oysters in half. Cook the oysters in boiling water for 1 minute; remove and drain. Shorten the cooking time if the oysters are small.

❷ Heat the wok then add 3 T. oil. Stir-fry ① until fragrant. Add oysters and stir lightly. Add green onions and ②; stir quickly over high heat until mixed well. Serve.

Oyster in Lemon Sauce

6 large oysters, live in shell
1 T. cooking wine

① { 1 T. lemon juice
1 t. grated ginger root
¼ t. salt
1 T. chopped green onions
dash of chili powder

❶ Thoroughly scrub the shells of the oysters under running water; drain. Use an awl to make a hole at 2/3 of the joint end of the shell. Insert a knife or screw driver into the hole until the adductor muscle is cut. Open the shells of the oysters (Figs. 1, 2). Cut the shellfish free and rinse it.

❷ Marinate the oysters in 1 T. cooking wine for 5 minutes; drain. Refrigerate the oysters on bottom shelf of refrigerator. Sprinkle with ① and serve.

■ Ingredients ① may be substituted with ketchup or mustard sauce.

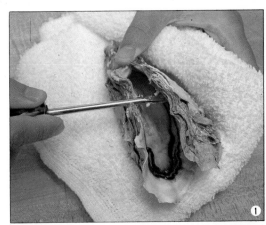

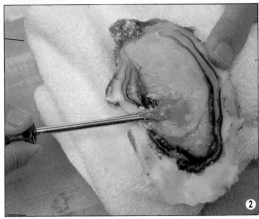

魚香鮮貝
Scallops with Fish Flavor

煎鮮貝
Fried Scallops

74

Scallops with Fish Flavor

10 large scallops (about 2/3 lb.)
① { ½ T. each: cooking wine, cornstarch
    ⅓ t. salt
    oil
② { 3 T. chopped green onions
    1 T. chopped ginger root
    ½ T. chopped garlic
    ½ t. chili paste
    1 c. mushrooms, cut in half
    12 slices cucumber
③ { 3 T. water
    ½ T. each: cooking wine, sugar, vinegar,
              soy sauce
    1 t. each: cornstarch, sesame oil
    ⅓ t. salt

❶ Cut the scallops crosswise in half (see photo below). Marinate them in ① for 30 minutes. Heat the wok then add oil for precooking. Stir-fry the scallops until cooked; remove. Remove the oil.
❷ Heat the wok then add 3 T. oil. Stir-fry ② until fragrant. Add mushrooms, cucumber; stir lightly. Add the scallops and ③ ; stir quickly until mixed well. Serve.
■ For an elegant presentation, this dish may be served in a noodle basket (see p. 149 of "Chinese Appetizers & Garnishes").

Fried Scallops

10 large scallops (about ⅔ lb.)
① the same as ingredients ① of "Scallops with Fish Flavor"
2 T. oil
② { 3 T. water
    1 T. oyster sauce
    ⅓ t. cornstarch
    sesame oil
    1 T. chopped green onions

❶ Clean scallops and pat then dry. Marinate the scallops in ① for 30 minutes.
❷ Heat the pan then add 2 T. oil. Fry the scallops over high heat until both sides are golden brown (about 3 minutes). Add ② and green onions; mix well quickly; serve.

Crispy Deep-fried Scallops

10 scallops (about ⅔ lb.)
① the same as ingredients ① of "Scallops with Fish Flavor"
② { 1 c. flour
    ¾ c. water
    1 T. oil
    ½ t. baking powder
    oil
    dipping sauce: Szechuan peppercorn salt or
                   ketchup.

❶ Cut the scallops crosswise in half. Marinate then in ① for 30 minutes. Mix ② into a paste.
❷ Heat the wok then add oil. Dip the scallops in the flour paste then deep-fry them until golden brown (about 3 minutes); remove. Serve with dipping sauce.

Frozen scallops may be used in these recipes. To make the deep-fried scallops crispier, add ⅓ t. baking soda when mixing scallops with ① .

生炒牛角蚌
Stir-fried Scallops (A)

清蒸牛角蚌
Steamed Scallops

Stir-fried Scallops (A)

12 live in shell scallops
① { ½ T. each: cooking wine, cornstarch
    ¼ t. salt
½ c. oil
② { 1 hot pepper, sliced
    6 pieces green onions, 1 inch long
    6 slices ginger root
    1 t. chopped garlic
③ { 6 slices carrot
    6 Chinese pea pods
    12 straw mushrooms
④ { 1½ T. water
    1 T. cooking wine
    1 t. each: sesame oil, cornstarch
    ⅓ t. salt

❶ Remove the scallops from the shells; remove their stomachs. Cut the scallops in half and marinate them in ① for 10 minutes.
❷ Heat the wok then add ½ c. oil. Stir-fry the scallops until cooked; remove. Remove the oil from the wok.
❸ Heat the wok then add 2 T. oil. Stir-fry ② until fragrant; add ③ and stir lightly. Add the scallops and ④, stir quickly until thoroughly mixed.

Steamed Scallops

12 live in shell scallops (see photo below)
① { 1 T. each: cooking wine, soy sauce
    1 t. sesame oil
    ⅓ t. salt
    dash of pepper
② { 1 T. shredded ginger root
    1 hot pepper, shredded
    ½ T. chopped garlic

● Remove the scallops from the shells; clean the scallops. Place each scallop in a shell; sprinkle with ① . Arrange a portion of ② on each shell. Steam the scallops over boiling water, over high heat, for 5 minutes or until cooked. Serve hot.

> Serving scallops in shells make an elegant presentation. If live scallops are not available, clams or frozen scallops may be used.

Stir-fried Scallops (B)

● Ingredients and steps are the same as for "Stir-fried Scallops (A)" except substitute fresh scallops for live in shell scallops.

生 炒 象 拔 蚌
Stir-fried Geoduck Clam

白 灼 象 拔 蚌
Boiled Geoduck Clam

Stir-fried Geoduck Clam

¾ lb. geoduck clam, remove from shell
3 T. oil
6 pieces green onion, 1 inch long
6 slices ginger root
① { 12 slices carrot
    ¾ c. straw mushrooms or button mushrooms,
       sliced
② { 3 T. water
    ½ T. cooking wine
    1 t. each: sesame oil, cornstarch
    ½ t. salt
    dash of pepper

❶ Slice the clam and cook it in boiling water for 25 seconds; remove.

❷ Heat the wok then add 3 T. oil. Stir-fry the green onions and ginger root until fragrant. Add ① and stir lightly. Add the clams then stir. Add ② ; stir quickly until mixed well.

■ See "Boiled Geoduck Clam" for basic preparation.

> Any kind of clams and scallops may substitute for geoduck clam.

Boiled Geoduck Clam

1 geoduck clam (about 2-3 lbs.)
① { 6 pieces green onions, 1 inch long
    6 slices ginger root
    3 garlic clove, mashed
② { 2 T. each: shredded ginger root,
              shredded green onions
    1 hot pepper, cut into pieces
    2½ T. each: soy sauce, stock
    dash of black pepper
2 c. stock or water
1 T. oil

❶ Remove and discard the shell and the stomach of the clam (Fig. 1). Plunge the clam in boiling water; remove the skin (Fig. 2). Cut the clam into thin slices (The clam to be used is about ⅓ of the entire weight). Mix ② together.

❷ Heat the wok then add 1 T. oil. Stir-Fry ① until fragrant. Add 2 c. stock and bring to a boil; remove ① . Cook the clam in boiling stock for 25 seconds; remove. Retain the liquid. Serve the clam with ② while it is still hot.

酒烹海瓜子
Simmered Clams in Cooking Wine

炒山瓜子
Stir-fried Clams

Simmered Clams in Cooking Wine

    1⅓ lbs. clams
    2   T. oil
① ⎧ 2   chopped green onions
    ⎨ ½   T. each: chopped ginger root,
    ⎩   chopped garlic
      ½   hot pepper, seeds removed, chopped
② ⎧ ⅓   c. cooking wine
    ⎩ ½   t. salt
③ ⎧ 1   t. cornstarch ⎫ mix
    ⎩ 1   T. water   ⎭
    2   T. chopped green onions
    1   T. chopped coriander

❶ Clean, wash and drain the clams (see p. 11).
❷ Heat the wok then add 2 T. oil. Stir-fry ① until fragrant. Add the clams; stir over high heat for 1 minute. Add ② and cover the wok; simmer for 3 minutes or until the shells open slightly. Add ③ to thicken; stir. Sprinkle with green onions and coriander.

> Any kind of clams may be used for clam recipes.

Simmered Shrimp in Cooking Wine

● Ingredients and steps are the same as for "Slimmered Clams in Cooking Wine" except substitute ⅔ lb. shrimp for clams.

Stir-fried Clams

    1⅓ lbs. clams
    3   T. oil
① ⎧ 2   T. chopped green onions
    ⎨ 1   T. each: chopped ginger root, chopped garlic
    ⎩ 1   hot pepper, sliced
② ⎧ 2½ T. each: cooking wine, soy sauce
    ⎨ 1   T. vinegar
    ⎩ ½   T. each: sugar, sesame oil
      ½   c. coriander

❶ Clean the clams (see p. 11).
❷ Heat the wok then add 3 T. oil. Stir-fry ① until fragrant. Add clams and stir quickly over high heat until the shells open slightly. Add ② and coriander; stir quickly and mix well. Serve.

Stir-fried Clam Meat

● Ingredients and steps are the same as for "Stir-fried Clams", except substitute clam meat or scallop meat for clams (Fig. 1).

Clams in Oyster Sauce

    1⅓ lbs. clams
    2   T. oil
① ⎧ 2   T. chopped green onions
    ⎨ ½   T. chopped ginger root
    ⎩ 1   hot pepper, chopped
② ⎧ 1½ T. each: cooking wine, oyster sauce
    ⎩ 1   t. cornstarch
      3   T. chopped green onions

❶ Clean the clams (see p. 11).
❷ Heat the wok then add 2 T. oil. Stir-fry ① until fragrant. Add the clams and stir-fry over high heat until the shells open slightly. Add ② and stir quickly to mix. Sprinkle with green onions and serve (Fig. 2).

海瓜子炒麵
Stir-fried Noodles with Clams

炒生蠔麵線
Stir-fried Noodle Strings
with Oysters

Stir-fried Noodles with Clams

- 2 lbs. thick noodles
- 3 T. oil
- 1 onion, shredded
- 1½ c. coarsely diced tomatoes
- 1 lb. clams
① {
- 2 T. soy sauce
- ⅔ T. sugar
- ½ t. salt
- dash of pepper
- 1 t. sesame oil
- 1 c. stock or water
}
② {
- 1 T. cornstarch
- 2 T. water
} mix
- 3 T. chopped green onions

❶ Release the sand from the clams (see p. 11) then clean them. Cook the noodles in boiling water; remove and drain.

❷ Heat the wok then add 3 T. oil. Stir-fry the onions then add the tomatoes; stir for 2 minutes. Add ① and the clams; bring to a boil. Add noodles and cook for 2 minutes. Add ② to thicken and stir lightly. Sprinkle with green onions.

■ Any kind of noodles may be used for this dish (see photo below).

Stir-fried Noodle Strings with Oysters

- ½ lb. oysters
- 3 T. oil
- ½ c. shredded beef, pork or chicken
① {
- 10 pieces green onions, 2 inches long
- ½ T. chopped garlic
}
② {
- 2 c. shredded cabbage
- ½ c. shredded carrot
- ¼ c. Chinese black mushrooms
}
- ⅔ lb. noodle strings
③ {
- 1½ T. cooking wine
- ½ t. salt
- dash of pepper
- ½ T. sesame oil
- ½ c. stock or water
}

❶ Clean the oysters; cut large ones in half. Plunge the noodle strings in boiling water; remove and rinse in cold water then drain.

❷ Heat the wok then add 3 T. oil. Stir-fry ① until fragrant; add beef and stir lightly. Add oysters and ② ;stir until the cabbage is soft. Add ③ ; bring to a boil then add noodle strings and stir for 1 minute.

■ Noodle strings should not be overcooked.

> Various ingredients are used in stir-frying noodles and noodle strings. Clams, oysters, shrimp, scallops or squid may be added to taste.

酥炸魷魚
Crispy Squid

魚香墨花
Stir-fried Cuttlefish

Crispy Squid

1 lb. squid (remove heads and foreign matter)
① {
½ T. cooking wine
½ t. salt
1 green onion (mashed)
2 slices ginger root
}
½ c. cornstarch
oil

- Clean the squid then cut them into rings (see photo below). Mix with ① ; then coat the squid with cornstarch. Heat the wok then add oil. Deep-fry the squid for 5 minutes or until golden brown; remove and serve with Szechuan peppercorn salt, ketchup or hot soy sauce.

> Squid and cuttlefish are the same kind of seafood. They may be used interchangeably.

Stir-fried Cuttlefish

⅔ lb. cuttlefish (remove heads and foreign matter)
① {
1 T. cornstarch
½ T. cooking wine
⅓ t. salt
½ egg white
}
½ c. oil
② {
1 T. each, chopped: green onions, ginger root, garlic clove
1 t. hot bean paste
}
5 water chestnuts, chopped
4 T. wood ears, chopped
③ {
2½ T. water
1½ T. oyster sauce or soy sauce
½ T. each: cooking wine, vinegar
1 t. each: sugar, cornstarch
}

❶ Clean the cuttlefish then cut them into pieces (see p. 13 for the method of cutting). Mix ① with cuttlefish.
❷ Heat the wok then add oil. Stir-fry the cuttlefish until they curl; remove. Remove the oil. Reheat the wok then add 1 T. oil. Stir-fry ② until fragrant. Add water chestnuts and wood ears; stir lightly. Add the cuttlefish; and ③ stir-fry over high heat. Mix well and serve.
■ Cuttlefish may be substituted with squid. Other ingredients such as Chinese pea pods, bamboo shoots, button mushrooms, celery, or carrot may be added to taste.

Stir-fried Cuttlefish with Asparagus

⅔ lb. cuttlefish (remove heads and foreign matter)
① the same as ingredient ① of "Stir-fried Cuttlefish"
½ c. oil
② {
6 pieces green onions, 1 inch long
6 slices ginger root
}
③ {
6 asparagus
12 slices bamboo shoot
12 button mushrooms
}
④ {
2 T. water
1 T. cooking wine
1 t. each: cornstarch, sesame oil
½ t. salt
dash of pepper
}

❶ Follow step ❶ of "Stir-fry Cuttlefish". Cut off the skin of the asparagus then cut them into 2 inches pieces. Blanch the asparagus in boiling water for 30 seconds; remove.
❷ Heat the wok then add oil. Stir-fry cuttlefish until they curl; remove.
❸ Heat the wok then add 2 T. oil. Stir-fry ② until fragrant; add ③ and stir lightly. Add cuttlefish and ④ ; stir-fry over high heat until mixed well. Serve.

薑汁魷魚
Squid in Ginger Sauce

時菜燴魷魚
Squid with Vegetables

Squid in Ginger Sauce

1	lb. squid (remove heads and foreign matter)
2	T. chopped ginger root
1	t. chopped garlic
1	hot pepper, sliced
① 3	T. soy sauce
1½	T. vinegar
1	T. sesame oil
½	T. sugar

OR

② 4½	T. vinegar
3	T. chopped ginger root
½	t. salt
½	T. fried sesame seeds

❶ Clean the squid then cut them lengthwise in center to butterfly them. Score the inside surface lengthwise and crosswise. Cut the squid into pieces (see p. 13 for the method of cutting). Blanch the pieces of squid in boiling water for 1 minute until they curl; remove. Place the squid on a serving plate; pour ① or ② over the squid. Sprinkle with sesame seeds. Serve hot or cold.

> Squid and cuttlefish are the same kind of seafood. They may be used interchangeably.

Stir-fried Squid

⅓	lb. squid (remove heads and foreign matter)
⅔	lb. celery
① 1	T. cooking wine
½	t. salt
	dash of pepper
3	T. oil

❶ Clean and shred the squid. Cut the celery into 4 inch pieces.
❷ Heat the wok then add 3 T. oil. Stir-fry the squid then add the celery and ① . Stir for about 1½ minutes until they are cooked.
■ Chinese leeks or asparagus may be used instead of celery.

Squid with Vegetables

⅔	lb. squid or cuttlefish (remove heads and foreign matter)
① ½	T. cooking wine
⅓	t. salt
2	T. oil
② 6	pieces green onions, 1 inch long
2	garlic clove, sliced
1	hot pepper, cut into pieces
③ 2	c. cucumber or choy sum, precooked and cut into pieces
2	c. white radish or broccoli, precooked and cut into pieces
3	Chinese black mushrooms (soak in water until soft)
④ 1½	c. stock
1¼	T. each: soy sauce, vinegar
½	T. each: sugar, cooking wine
½	t. salt
⑤ 2½	T. cornstarch } mix
4	T. water

❶ Clean the squid then pat then dry. Score the inside surface lengthwise and crosswise then cut the squid into pieces. Add ① to the squid and mix.
❷ Heat the wok then add 2 T. oil. Stir-fry the pieces of squid over high heat until they curl; remove.
❸ Clean the wok then reheat it; add 3 T. oil. Stir-fry ② until fragrant. Add ③ ; stir lightly then add ④ . Bring to a boil then add the squid. Add ⑤ to thicken; stir. Sesame oil and coriander may be added to taste.
■ Peel cucumber and remove seeds before cutting it into pieces. Broccoli should be cut into pieces and washed before using (see photo below).

腐皮海鮮捲
Bean Curd Rolls with Seafood

炸 魚 餅
Fried Fish Cake

Bean Curd Rolls with Seafood

3   bean curd skins or egg sheets (6" x 8")
① ⎰ ½   lb. fish cake
  ⎱ ¼   lb. ground meat, beef or pork
  ⎰ 1   T. each: cooking wine, sugar
  ⎱ dash of salt and pepper
  dash of salt
② ⎰ 12   medium size shrimp
  ⎱ 1½   sausage or ham   ⎱ divide into
  ⎰ 4   T. shredded carrot   ⎰ 3 portions
  ⎱ ½   lb. spinich or Chinese leeks
③ ⎰ 1   egg ⎱ mix
  ⎱ 2   T. flour ⎰
  oil

❶ Mix ① together; divide it into 3 portions. Add dash of salt to the shrimp of ② ; let stand. Cut one sausage lengthwise into 4 strips (1½ sausage can be cut into 6 strips.)

❷ Place one portion of ① on a bean curd skin. Place one portion of ② on the center of ① (see photo below). Roll up the skin sheet to form a baton. Use the same steps to prepare the other rolls.

❸ Heat the wok then add oil (see p. 7 for deep-frying). Coat the bean curd rolls with ③ ; deep-fry them over low heat for 5 minutes. Turn the heat to high; deep-fry the bean curd rolls for 2 minutes or until golden brown. Remove the rolls then cut them into serving pieces. Serve with Szechuan peppercorn salt, ketchup, barbecue sauce or hot soy sauce.

■ Store bought fish cake is salted, therefore, salt in ingredients ① should only be added to taste.

■ The ingredients in ② may be substituted with cuttlefish, bamboo shoots or Chinese black mushrooms, etc.

Fried Fish Cake

① ⎰ ½   lb. fish cake
  ⎱ ½   lb. ground meat, beef or pork
  ⎰ 1   onion, chopped
  ⎱ ½   c. chopped carrot
② ⎰ 1½   T. sugar
  ⎰ 1   T. cooking wine
  ⎰ 1   t. sesame oil
  ⎱ ⅓   t. salt
  dash of pepper
  ⎰ 2   T. cornstarch
  2   c. bread crumbs
  oil

❶ To prepare filling: Mix fish cake, ground meat, ① and ② thoroughly.

❷ Form the fish cake into 30 fish balls. Coat the fish balls with bread crumbs. Flatten each ball with palm of hand.

❸ Heat the wok then add oil. Deep-fry the fish cake for 3 or 4 minutes or until golden brown; remove. Serve with Szechuan peppercorn salt, ketchup, barbecue sauce or hot soy sauce.

■ Ingredients in ① may be substituted with bamboo shoots, water chestnuts, or Chinese black mushrooms, etc.

Fish Rolls

½   lb. fish cake
½   lb. ground meat, beef or pork
①   the same as ingredient ① of "Fried Fish Cake"
②   the same as ingredient ② of "Fried Fish Cake"
6   bean curd skin (6" x 8")
oil

❶ To prepare filling: Mix fish cake, ground meat, ① and ② thoroughly.

❷ Divide the filling into 6 portions. Put one portion of filling on the center of a bean curd skin. Roll the bean curd to form a baton.

❸ Heat the wok then add oil. Deep-fry the fish rolls over low heat for 4 mintues then turn the heat to high; continue frying for 2 minutes or until crispy. Remove and drain. Cut the fish rolls into serving pieces. Serve with ketchup, Szechuan peppercorn salt or barbecue sauce.

■ Egg sheet, nori or egg roll skin may be substituted for bean curd skin.

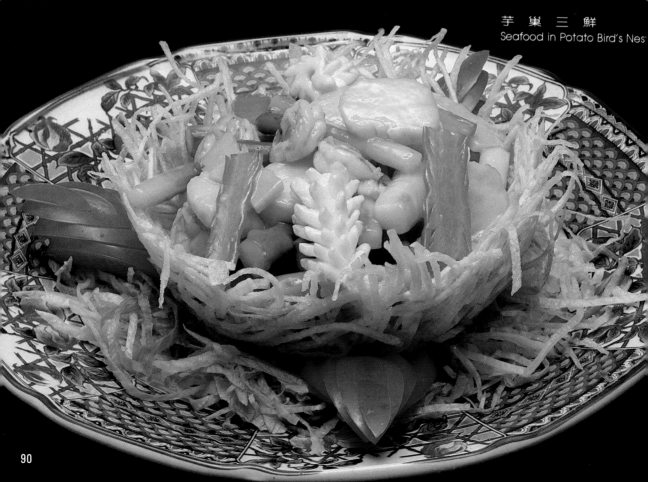

芋 巢 三 鮮
Seafood in Potato Bird's Nest

Seafood Salad

12 slices squid
6   fresh scallops, sliced
12 medium shrimp
1   lb. green asparagus, cut off hard skin, cut into 2 inch lengths
4   T. mayonnaise

❶ Cook the asparagus over boiling water for 3 minutes; remove. Rinse in cold water until cool; drain and place on a serving plate.

❷ Bring water to a boil. Cook squid, scallops and shrimp in the water for 1½ minutes; remove and drain. Place the ingredients on top of the asparagus. Spread mayonnaise over the squid, scallops and shrimp; serve.

■ Other kinds of seafood and vegetable may be used.

■ This dish may be served in a potato bird's nest.

Seafood in Potato Bird's Nest

12 slices squid
6   fresh scallops, sliced   ① { 1 T. cornstarch
12 medium shrimp   ½ T. cooking wine
oil   ⅓ t. salt
6   pieces green onions, 1 inch long
6   slices ginger root
② { 12 pieces fresh asparagus, 2 inches long, precooked
    12 slices each, precooked: carrot, bamboo shoot
1   potato bird's nest
  { 3   T. water
    ½ T. cooking wine
③ { 1   t. each: sugar, sesame oil, cornstarch
    ½ t. salt
  { dash of black pepper

❶ Prepare scallops, shrimp and squid (see pps. 12, 13); mix with ① .

❷ Heat the wok and add ½ cup oil. Stir-fry the squid, scallops and shrimp until cooked; remove. Remove the oil. Put 2 T. oil in the wok and stir-fry green onions and ginger root until fragrant. Add ② and stir lightly. Add the squid, scallops, shrimp and ③ ; stir quickly over high heat until mixed well. Remove and place in the bird's nest.

■ **To prepare potato bird's nest:** Soak 2 cups shredded potatoes in water for about one hour (change water 2 or 3 times); remove and drain (see Fig. 1). Mix the potatoes with 4 T. cornstarch. Grease a strainer with oil arrange the shredded potatoes on the strainer. Put another strainer on the top of the potatoes (see Fig. 2). Deep-fry the potatoes until cooked to form a bird's nest.

寧汁拌帶芽
Seaweed in Lemon Juice Salad

紙 包 海 鮮
Baked Seafood in
Foil Packets

Seaweed
...Salad

r 30
red
or 2

late;
erate
well;

y be

d, the
d be
g.

Baked Seafood
in Foil Packets

24	medium shrimp	
⅔	lb. oysters	

① {
1 T. cooking wine
½ t. salt
dash of pepper
}

③ {
3 T. stock or water
1 T. cooking wine
½ T. sesame oil
½ t. salt
}

② {
12 button mushrooms or straw mushrooms
12 slices each: bamboo shoot, carrot
¼ lb. spinach
}

6 sheets aluminum foil (12″ x 12″)

❶ Remove the shells of the shrimp and leave the tails intact; remove the dark vein. Wash the shrimp and oysters in water; drain. Cut the large oysters in half. Mix the shrimp and oysters with ① ; marinate for 10 minutes. Mix ③ together.

❷ To arrange the six packets, put one portion of each, as listed on an aluminum sheet: ingredient ② , shrimp, oysters, and ③ (see Fig. 1 below). Wrap the foil into a swan-like shape or square (see Fig. 2 below). Use the same steps to prepare the remaining sheets.

❸ Preheat oven to 500°F. Bake the wrapped seafood for 18 minutes. Serve the seafood packets; open the packet when ready to serve.

■ Shrimp and oysters may be substituted with fillet, dried scallops, etc. Ingredients in ② may be substituted with zucchini, celery and Chinese black mushrooms.

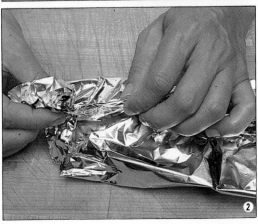

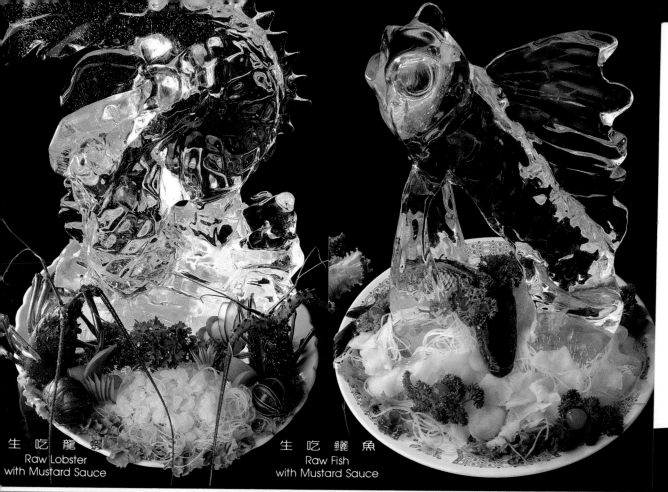

生 吃 龍 蝦
Raw Lobster
with Mustard Sauce

生 吃 鱺 魚
Raw Fish
with Mustard Sauce

生 吃 九 孔
Raw Abalone with Mustard Sauce

Raw Lobster
with Mustard Sauce

```
2   lbs. live in shell lobster
2   c. shredded white radish
¼   c. shredded carrots
```
① { mustard sauce
    2   T. soy sauce } dipping sauce

❶ Use a cloth or glove to hold the head of the lobster. Cut at the joint of the head and the body; twist off the head and pull the head and the body apart (use cloth to avoid hurting fingers). Cut from the belly of the lobster; remove the shell and pull the meat out. Cut the lobster meat into pieces then rinse it in ice water for about 5 minutes to make it crunchy.

❷ Soak the white radish and the carrots in ice water for about 10 minutes; remove and drain. Place the lobster on a bed of shredded white radish and carrots. Serve with ①

■ To make mustard sauce: Thoroughly mix 1½ T. dried mustard and 1 T. water; cover in an airtight container and let stand for 10 minutes.

■ To shred the white radish: Use the middle section of a white radish. Pare the radish then trim it into a baton-like shape. Hold a cleaver or knife parallel to the radish. Cut a long continuous sheet around the length of the radish (Fig. 1). Roll up the radish sheet then shred it (Fig 2). OR use a grater to shred the radish.

Raw Fish
with Mustard Sauce

Ingredients are the same as for "Raw Lobster with Mustard Sauce" except substitute live or fresh sea fish (about 2 lbs. whole fish or 1 lb. fish meat) for lobster.

❶ Prepare and clean the fish. Fillet the fish and cut it into pieces. Refrigerate for at least 1 hour.

❷ Follow step ❷ of "Raw Lobster with Mustard Sauce".

■ Yellowtail, mackerel, tuna, salmon, or sea bass may be used in this recipe.

Raw Abalone
with Mustard Sauce

Ingredients are the same as for "Raw Lobster with Mustard Sauce" except substitute 1 abalone for 2 lbs. live lobster.

❶ Pry the whole foot muscle from the shell; remove and discard the stomach. Clean the abalone then slice it (see p. 71). Refrigerate for at least 1 hour.

❷ The same as step ❷ of "Raw Lobster with Mustard Sauce".

■ The meat of the small abalone is more tender than the meat of large abalone.

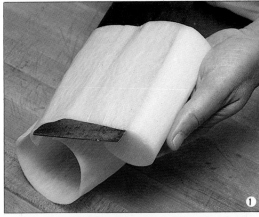

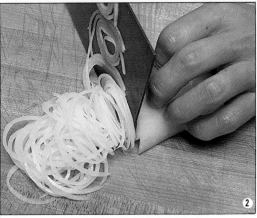

鮑 魚 蒸 蛋
Steamed Eggs with
Abalone

Steamed Eggs with Assorted Seafood

```
1    crab, cut into pieces
6    each: clams, shrimp
6    each: abalone, sea cucumbers
3    oz. oysters
3    large eggs
①   ⎧1    T. cooking wine
    ⎪1    t. salt
    ⎨1    t. sesame oil
    ⎩3½  c. stock or water
②   ⎧½    T. cooking wine
    ⎨½    t. salt
    ⎩2    c. stock
③   ⎰1⅓  T. cornstarch⎱ mix
    ⎱2    T. water    ⎰
2    T. chopped green onions
```

❶ Clean all seafood (see pps. 11, 12); put in a heatproof bowl. Beat the eggs and mix with ① ; pour them into the bowl. Boil water in a pan; steam the bowl over low heat for 20 minutes until the eggs are done.

❷ Bring ② to a boil then add ③ to thicken; stir lightly. Pour this mixture over the eggs; sprinkle with green onions and serve.

Family-style Steamed Eggs

```
4    T. chopped ham or chopped fish cake
4    T. chopped celery
3    large eggs
①, ② and ③ are the same as ingredients ①,
    ② and ③ of "Steamed Eggs with
    Assorted Seafood".
```

● Steps are the same as for "Steamed Eggs with Assorted Seafood".

Steamed Eggs with Abalone

```
12   slices abalone
½    lb. shrimp paste or fish cake
3    salty egg yolks
24   shreds of black mushrooms
3    large eggs
①, ② and ③ are the same as ingredients ①, ②
    and ③ of "Steamed Eggs with Assorted Seafood"
```

❶ Divide the shrimp paste into 12 portions. Cut each salty egg yolk into four pieces; roll them into small balls. Sprinkle an abalone slice with a little cornstarch. Spread a portion of shrimp paste on top of the abalone. Put a salty egg yolk ball on the center of the shrimp paste; arrange two shreds of black mushroom on two sides. Follow the same procedure for the remaining portions. (Abalone may be substituted with a medium size shrimp. Cut the shrimp at the back to butterfly. Spread shrimp paste on the shrimp and make the center a little concave. Put a quail egg on the center as a substitute for salty egg yolk.).

❷ Beat the eggs and mix with ① ; pour into a heatproof bowl. Boil water in a pan; steam over low heat for 12 minutes or until the egg is half-done. Arrange the abalone in the bowl; continue to steam over low heat for 8 minutes or until the egg is cooked.

❸ Bring ② to a boil then thicken with ③ ; stir lightly. Gently pour this mixture on the egg and sprinkle with green onions. This dish may be served as a soup.

Steamed Eggs with Clams

```
12   clams
coriander
3    large eggs
①, ②, and ③ are the same as ingredients ①, ②,
    and ③ of "Steamed Eggs with Assorted Seafood"
```

● Steps are the same as for "Steamed Eggs with Assorted Seafood".

---

❶ Various ingredients are used in steaming eggs. Only one or many ingredients may be used. The ingredients may be divided into several portions and put into small bowls to make single servings. If an electric roasting pan is used, steam the eggs at 225°F (see photo below). Steaming time may vary depending on the kind of container used. Test for doneness during steaming by inserting a toothpick in the center of the egg. If the toothpick is clean when removed the egg is cooked.

❷ If canned stock is used In ingredient ① and ② , reduce the salt by ¼ t. for each can of stock used.

生炒蛤蜊肉
Stir-fried
Clam Meat

海鮮玉米湯
Seafood and Corn Soup

Stir-fried Clam Meat

2 lbs. clams
½ lb. spinach, cut into 4 inch lengths
① {
6 pieces green onions, 1 inch long
6 slices ginger root
1 hot red pepper, sliced
}
② {
½ c. button mushrooms
1 green pepper, cut into pieces
}
③ {
1 T. cooking wine
1 t. sesame oil
½ t. salt
dash of pepper
4 T. clam liquid, reserved from step
1 t. cornstarch
}
3 T. oil

❶ Release the sand from the clams (see p. 11). Scrub the shells and clean them. Cook the clams in 1 c. boiling water until the shells open slightly; remove and save the liquid. Remove the clams from their shells.

❷ Stir-fry the spinach with ¼ t. salt until cooked; drain and put on a plate.

❸ Heat the wok then add 3 T. oil. Stir-fry ① until fragrant; add ② and stir lightly. Add the clams and ③ ; stir quickly over high heat until mixed well. Place the clams on the spinach and serve. The shells may be arranged around the plate as a garnish; serve.

■ Ingredients in ② may be substituted with onion, celery, Chinese black mushrooms, bamboo shoots, carrots or water chestnuts.

Clam Soup

1 lb. clams
① {
6 c. water
1 T. cooking wine
1¼ t. salt
dash of pepper
1½ T. shredded ginger root
}
12 Chinese pea pods
6 pieces green onions, 1 inch long

❶ Release the sand from the clams (see p. 11). Scrub the shells and clean them.

❷ Bring ① to a boil. Cook clams in ① until the shells open lightly. Add pea pods and green onions; bring to a boil again. Serve.

■ Bean threads may be added to the soup. Bean threads should be soaked in water until soft before using.

Seafood and Corn Soup

12 medium shrimp
3 scallops
6 clams
① {
1 can creamed corn
5 c. stock or water
1½ T. cooking wine
1¼ t. salt
dash of pepper
}
② {
3 T. cornstarch
4 T. water
1 T. chopped green onions
}

❶ Slice the scallops. Release the sand from the clams (see p. 11); scrub the shells and clean them.

❷ Bring ① to a boil. Add clams, shrimp and scallops; bring to a boil again. Add ② to thicken; stir. Sprinkle with green onions and serve.

■ Various seafoods may be used in this soup.

海產火鍋
Seafood Fire Pot

冬瓜蟹湯
Winter Squash and Crab Soup

Seafood Fire Pot

① {
- 1   crab, cut into pieces
- ⅓   lb. oysters
- 6   slices each: sea cucumber, squid, fillet
- 6   large shrimp
- 6   clams
- 6   slices fish cake
}

② {
- ½   lb. nappa cabbage, cut into pieces
- 1   tomato, cut into pieces
- 2   slices ginger root
- ¼   c. pickled mustard cabbage or Szechuan pickled mustard greens
}

③ {
- 6   c. stock
- 2   T. cooking wine
- 1½   t. salt
- sesame oil
- dash of pepper
}

④ {
- 3   T. soy sauce
- 1   T. chopped ginger root
- 1   hot pepper, sliced
}

❶ Put ③ in fire pot and bring to a boil. Add ② and bring to a boil again. Arrange ① on a plate (These raw ingredients are placed in the fire pot and cook while other ingredients are removed and eaten.). Place selections from ingredients ① in the fire pot. Remove selections from fire pot and dip them in ④ before eating.
OR

❷ Bring ③ to a boil. Add ② and bring to a boil again; add ①. Cover the fire pot and cook until all the ingredients are cooked then serve (see photo below).

■ Fish balls, shrimp balls, Chinese black mushrooms, spinach, Chinese pea pods, bean threads, beef or pork may be added to taste.

Winter Squash and Crab Soup

- 2   lbs. crabs

① {
- ½   T. cooking wine
- ½   t. salt
- 2   T. cornstarch
}
- oil

② {
- 12   pieces winter squash
- 1   chicken leg, cut into pieces
- 3   Chinese black mushrooms, cut in half
- 3   bok choy, cut in half
}

③ {
- 6   c. stock
- 1   T. cooking wine
- 1   T. chopped garlic
- ½   T. chopped ginger root
- 1½   t. salt
- 1   t. sesame oil
}

❶ Clean the crabs and cut them into pieces (see p. 11). Marinate them in ①. Drain the crabs and coat them with cornstarch before frying.

❷ Heat the wok then add oil. Deep-fry the crabs over high heat for 3 minutes or until golden brown; remove.

❸ Bring ③ to a boil; add ② and the crabs; bring to a boil again. Remove the scum and turn the heat to low; cook for 10 minutes or until the winter squash is soft. Add the bok choy; continue cooking for 3 minutes. Sprinkle with sesame oil and serve.

■ Pare the winter squash and remove the seeds. Cut the squash into pieces (see Figs. 1, 2).

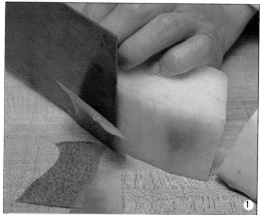

UTENSILS USED TO PREPARE CHINESE DISHES

1 Wok (iron)

Diameter 12½"
Weight 2¼ lbs.

Stir-fry: Heat the wok then add oil. Add the ingredients and stir-fry. The width and the depth of the wok make stir-frying easy.

Deep-fry: The concave shape of the wok makes it easy to adjust the amount of oil according to the amount of the ingredients.

2 Strainer (stainless steel)

Small: Diameter 6½", Weight ½ lb.
Medium: Diameter 8¼", Weight ¾ lb.

Strainer is useful to remove the ingredients after deep-frying.

Strainer is also useful for removing cooked noodles.

③ Spatula (stainless steel)

Length 12½"
Weight ¼ lb.

④ Thin Cleaver (stainless steel)

Length 11"
Weight ⅔ lb.

The thin cleaver is used to slice and shred.

⑤ Gas Burner (iron)

Diameter 12"
Weight 19 lbs.
This burner provides greater heat.

⑥ Thick Cleaver (stainless steel)

Length 11"
Weight 1⅓ lbs.

The thick cleaver is used to cut bones and other hard materials.

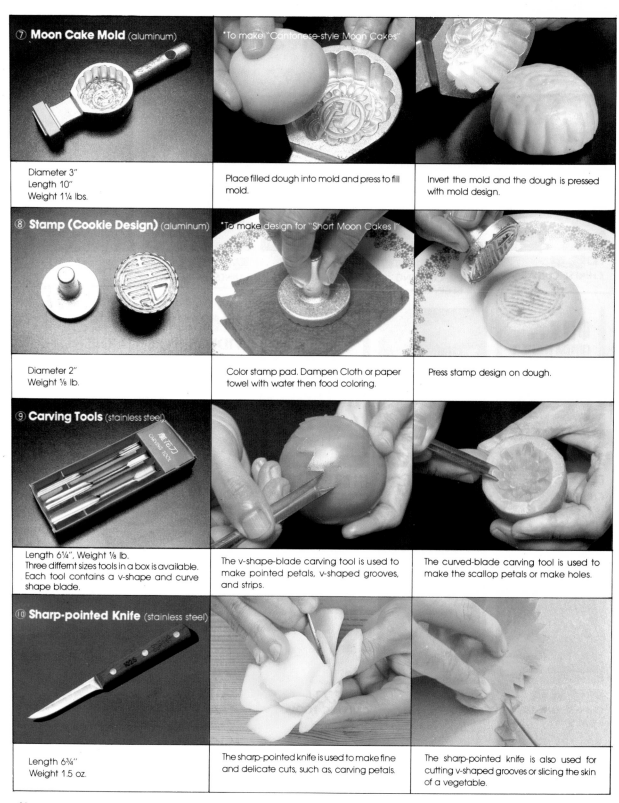

⑦ **Moon Cake Mold** (aluminum)

Diameter 3″
Length 10″
Weight 1¼ lbs.

*To make "Cantonese-style Moon Cakes"

Place filled dough into mold and press to fill mold.

Invert the mold and the dough is pressed with mold design.

⑧ **Stamp (Cookie Design)** (aluminum)

Diameter 2″
Weight ⅛ lb.

*To make design for "Short Moon Cakes I"

Color stamp pad. Dampen Cloth or paper towel with water then food coloring.

Press stamp design on dough.

⑨ **Carving Tools** (stainless steel)

Length 6¼″, Weight ⅛ lb.
Three differnt sizes tools in a box is available. Each tool contains a v-shape and curve shape blade.

The v-shape-blade carving tool is used to make pointed petals, v-shaped grooves, and strips.

The curved-blade carving tool is used to make the scallop petals or make holes.

⑩ **Sharp-pointed Knife** (stainless steel)

Length 6¾″
Weight 1.5 oz.

The sharp-pointed knife is used to make fine and delicate cuts, such as, carving petals.

The sharp-pointed knife is also used for cutting v-shaped grooves or slicing the skin of a vegetable.

*See p. 102 of "Chinese Cooking for Beginners" for "Cantonese-style Moon Cakes".
*See p. 103 of "Chinese Cooking for Beginners" for "Short Moon Cakes I".

CHINESE SEAFOOD

WEI-CHUAN'S COOKBOOK

Author: Huang Su-Huei
Published by: Huang Su-Huei
Distributed by: Sun-Chuan Publishing Co., Ltd.
2nd Fl., 28, Section 4, Jen Ai Rd.
Taipei, Taiwan, R.O.C.
Phone: 702-1148-9   Fax. 704-2729

Wei-Chuan's Cooking
(Publisher and Book Seller)
1455 Monterey Pass Rd., #110
Monterey Park, CA 91754
Phone: (213) 261-3880, 261-3878

1st Printing: August 1984
4th Printing: May 1988

ISBN: 0-941676-09-9